a CHARITABLE DISCOURSE

talking about the things that divide us

Dan BOONE

Nyack College - Baliey Library
One South Blvd.
Nyack, NY 10960

BEACON HILL PRESS
OF KANSAS CITY

Copyright 2010 by Dan Boone and Beacon Hill Press of Kansas City

ISBN 978-0-8341-2565-0

Cover Design: Arthur Cherry
Interior Design: Sharon Page

All Scripture quotations not otherwise designated are from the *New Revised Standard Version* (NRSV) of the Bible, copyright 1989 by the Division of Christian Education of the National Council of the Churches of Christ in the USA. Used by permission. All rights reserved.

Scriptures marked NIV are from the *Holy Bible: New International Version*® (NIV®). Copyright © 1973, 1978, 1984 by Biblica, Inc.™ Used by permission of Zondervan. All rights reserved worldwide. www.zondervan.com.

Library of Congress Cataloging-in-Publication Data

Boone, Dan, 1952-
A charitable discourse : talking about the things that divide us / Dan Boone.
p. c.m.
Includes bibliographical references.
ISBN 978-0-8341-2565-0 (pbk.)
1. Theology, Doctrinal—Popular works. 2. Christian life—Nazarene authors. I. Title.
BT77.B66 2010
287.9'9—dc22

2010045179

10 9 8 7 6 5 4 3 2 1

#676727523

Dedicated to
the students of
Trevecca Nazarene University.

You make me hope.

In essentials, unity;
in nonessentials, liberty;
in all things, charity.[1]

CONTENTS

PREFACE

In Defense of Fools

Fools rush in where angels fear to tread.[1]

Abraham Lincoln was possessed of great practical wisdom, the proverbial kind. He is reputed to have said, "Better to remain silent and be thought a fool, than to speak out and remove all doubt."[2] Others have offered the same type of wisdom. "Listen twice, speak once. That's why God gave us two ears and one tongue." "Preach the gospel at all times. If necessary, use words."[3] Having spoken too early and too often, I wish I had heeded these friends.

The accumulated wisdom of humans leans heavily to the side of reflective silence on issues of complexity and controversy. Those who dive into the deep end of this pool risk their reputations. When multiple opinions exist, there are sure to be sharks in the pool waiting for foolish divers who know no better than to jackknife into human disagreement.

So we stay quiet. About the young teen that everyone suspects to be homosexually oriented. About the blue state/red state divide that politicizes even geography. About social drinking in churches devoted to total abstinence. About creation theories in a world of scientific discovery. About end-of-the-world scenarios when a resident apocalyptic expert is present. About premarital sex when the couple about to be wed at the church altar are living together. About the use of religious power to extort money from soft-hearted people. About global warming when the radical radio guys have it all figured as a Democratic hoax. About latent racism in the church board election. About women preachers. About the emerging church.

We stay quiet, because Christians disagree about these things. And the younger generation watching us stays quiet too. Sadly, they may never hear a caring, thoughtful conversation on these topics between Christians with different perspectives. And when all they hear is opinionated posturing, how can they mature?

Mr. Everett Whittington was the Sunday school superintendent in my first pastorate at New Salem, Mississippi. I was only sixteen, and he was about eighty. The little country church at the end of the gravel road could get hot as blazes in the humid summer South. I preached to my little congregation of ten while standing six inches under a naked hundred-watt bulb dangling from a wire in the ceiling. I've always wondered if this was the beginning of a bald spot about the size of a light bulb's heat pattern. Red wasps circled the bulb as I preached. The heat attracted them. I was always cautious about breathing deeply or gesturing liberally.

A local businessman heard of our "heated" summer services and graciously donated an air conditioner for the church sanctuary. I was elated. When I presented the gift to the church board, Mr. Everett immediately staked his ground. "I'm agin it!" And with that, the discussion was ended. I brought it up a few more times and finally got to the bottom of his opposition. Apparently air-conditioning was in some way an accommodation to the prevailing evil culture. His opposition was summarized: "My Bible says, '*The morning air of the Lord will cool the sanctuary.*'" I was too young to realize that there is no verse in the Bible that says this. He was probably correct in saying that this was a verse in *his* Bible—his authoritative interpretation of the way the world functions. With his mind made up, nothing else mattered—not the comfort of worshippers, the welcome to new friends, the gift of the businessman, the leadership of the young pastor, the majority vote of the board. He was decided on the issue, and anyone who brought up the topic was not his friend.

Based on the vote of the board (two to one), we accepted the gift of the air conditioner, had it installed, and enjoyed a much less heated worship experience. But Mr. Everett left the church. Over an air conditioner, I lost 10 percent of my church and a third of my church board. Time healed the issue, and Mr. Everett returned, only to volunteer to come early and turn the air conditioner on to cool things down before everyone arrived.

I wonder if Mr. Everett knew the origin of his deeply held convictions. I doubt he had seriously talked about the issue with anyone. An air-conditioning prejudice had developed in his thought patterns across years and crystallized in a moment of decision. Can you imagine a country church that bowed year after year to his silent/threatening opposition to air-conditioning? *Generations of youth shaped by sweaty worship as the only one, true kind of worship. Real religion is the perspiring kind. If you can't stand the heated preaching, get out of the pewed kitchen. Good preaching defined by wet suits and sweat-soaked handkerchiefs.* Silly, I know. But this is how generations are shaped when the unspoken conclusions of the church are passed down only in cliché, evil characterization, judgment, and punishment of dissent. I'm not sure who is worse off—the generation that stays to be warped or the generation that walks away from the church in protest over this silent dishonesty.

Much later in my pastoral career, I came across Mr. Everett Whittington's clone—younger and more educated, but cut from the same cloth. I was pastor of a college campus church and was preaching a series on homosexuality. The "new" Mr. Everett informed me that I didn't need to trouble the congregation with this topic because "we don't have any of them around here, and if we do, they aren't here long." The unspoken opinion of his culture was to deny the very existence of these troubled students and to speak of their sexual orientation as if it did not exist. Thankfully, this Mr. Everett represented a minority opinion. The outpouring of letters from students struggling with sexual orientation assured me that they were present and wanting conversation. I have kept their letters to this day as a reminder that the ones most harmed by the silence of the church are those being spoken about, but seldom with.

Leaders who venture into controversial issues are seldom given the keys to institutional leadership. We prefer safe leaders who neither raise discomforting issues nor call the community to the painful task of revealing our biases. We prefer a theology whose answer to everything difficult is one quick trip to the altar followed by a testimony of resolution and conformity. We want to be made to feel better quickly, not taken into the bowels of difficulty. Life is hard enough without adding controversy to discipleship.

I write this book with deep appreciation for those who have suffered in their brave venture into these difficult issues. They have scars to show and stories to tell, but their platform for show-and-tell has been taken from them long ago by those who wished life to be easier. They are the heirs of the apostle Paul, who wrote about sexual ethics, lawsuits between believers, arguments between two church women, participation in pagan rituals, misuse of religious authority, refusal to work for a living, and legalism. Most of the letters of the Newer Testament are ours because Paul dared to rush in where angels feared to tread. He brought gossiped issues front and center. He named the persons involved and chronicled their positions. And he opened himself to all kinds of accusations—big talk, little power; in it for the money; anti-establishment. I'm guessing they also called him a liberal. That seems to end most Christian conversations.

This year I enter my twenty-fifth year of service to Christ on a Christian college campus—twenty as pastor and five as a college president. The generation now in college demands a conversation on ethical issues. And they will not sit still for long lectures without the chance to converse. They have thought about these things. They are embroiled in these issues. And they are not arrogant. They are willing to hear wise counsel and informed opinion. And lacking it, they will leave the church in search of a community where honest discourse is practiced.

This book is divided into three sections. In section one, I address the practices that prevent honest, charitable discourse. Beginning with the negative is my attempt to describe where we currently are. Section two surveys seven controversial issues and offers ways that Christians might talk together. Section three is our way forward—the doctrine of perfect love found in the Trinity and in the sanctifying work of the Spirit in the church.

One of the means of grace, according to John Wesley, is holy conversation. It is the practice of Spirit-guided listening to one another, discerning the ways of God, consulting Scripture, using our God-given reason, respecting the value of time-honored tradition, and speaking truthfully without fear of reprisal. In this atmosphere saints are made. I have belonged to a few communities like this. They have sanctified me by their gracious way of conversing. They were not afraid of controversy or complexity. Maybe they were fools—but in the way of the apostle Paul, fools for Christ.

With hope of resurrection,
Dan Boone
Easter 2010

ACKNOWLEDGMENTS

I wish to thank several friends who have allowed me to include their work in the book.

Dr. Tom Noble provided notes from a 2010 address to church leaders. You will find his footprints in the discussion on science and religion and in the chapters dealing with the emerging church. Footnotes identify his significant contributions. He is currently working on a systematic theology that will be a blessing to the church.

I must also thank an anonymous pastor whose pain in dealing with the issue of the emerging church connected us. I have used that individual's letters with permission but have shielded his/her identity out of respect for a congregation and pastor who have already had more press than they desire. Pastors like this make me want to believe in cloning.

My friend and mentor, Dr. William Greathouse, read the entire manuscript and urged me to publish it. His encouragement was the tipping point for daring to drag a wonderful university into the crosshairs of these debates. He believed the church needed to hear this.

I am grateful to Trevecca Nazarene University for the opportunity to work among a generation of students who are world changers. They put my generation to shame with their willingness to go anywhere for God. The impetus for this book came from a regular yearly chapel series on "hot potatoes." I am grateful for the encouragement of our university chaplain, Dr. Tim Green. Thanks to the students of Trevecca for their penetrating questions, which are scattered throughout the book. I long for them to embrace the world and its difficult issues with a Christian perspective. This book is dedicated to the students of Trevecca Nazarene University.

I am also grateful to Judge Charles Davis, chair of the board of trustees of Trevecca Nazarene University. His friendship in leading a Christian university is like that of a Christian brother. He read the manuscript and offered insightful help.

And there is my family. My parents are in the final chapter of their lives. Dad is eighty-seven. Mom is living with Alzheimer's. I see fear in her eyes each time we talk as the world she remembers is making its exit. They will not be here much longer. We don't agree on everything. But I love these two people for whom I have enormous gratitude and appreciation. Their little church, once among the strongest in the city, has declined to about seventy. The world has passed them by, and most of my generation has left their church for other denominations. It is a church that could not keep its young. That is part of my motivation in writing this book. The other part is the three families that Denise and I call our children. Our three daughters are married to wonderful Christian men and have given us four grandchildren. I want them to have a church that is willing to ask the hard questions in a spirit of charitable discourse.

Finally, God's thumb in the back would not go away. My life would no doubt be simpler flying under the radar of these divisive issues. To have my opinions in print is all the fodder dissenters need to make weapons of mass destruction. But I am reminded of the essence of sanctification: having died with Christ, we are made alive in Christ. Ruben Welch preached a sermon decades ago on the freedom of Jesus. He said that when we come to the place where we don't have to survive, we are free to do what pleases God. We are freed from defensiveness for honest conversation. We are free from fear for learning. We are free from an enemy-centered life for loving.

May God grant to me such glorious freedom.

—Dan Boone

Opening of the fall semester at Trevecca, 2010

section 1

JIHAD IN THE CHURCH

Why don't we talk more about controversial issues in the church? Why are we quieter than talk radio hosts and news entertainment folks? They tell us who did it, why, and what they meant by it. They actually say more than they know. And we say so much less than we believe.

Maybe we are afraid of appearing uninformed on an issue. After all, lack of intelligence seems to be one of America's greatest sins. It is quite humbling to say, "I don't know. What do you think?" Maybe we are afraid of the doubts that reside in our own questions. Maybe we are afraid that the answers may overturn our fixed worldviews or obligate us. Maybe we have not used our thought muscles on complex issues for a long time.

But maybe we just want to get along. We are afraid of challenging anyone or asking them to explain what they deeply believe. We don't want to become their enemy. We are afraid.

History is rich with ways of dealing with the enemy. From holy war in the Old Testament to the dungeon of the Spanish Inquisition to the Salem witch trials, we have always had ways of dealing with folks not like us. Today, we have religious fundamentalism of the violent and not-so-violent type. Central to this way of thinking is the creation of an enemy.

In a world where money, politics, and religion are center stage, there are always enemies being made. In each contest, there is a path to victory. With money, the one with the most wins. The poor loser goes home with less in his or her pocket. In politics, the party with the most votes wins. The defeated go home and cry in their milk. In religion, however, defeat is never quite enough. The enemy must be destroyed because they represent an allegiance to an "other" way. If they are right, it calls for a readjustment of one's worldview. Thus total annihilation is necessary. Holy war/divine judgment is the means and method of destroying the enemy. And lest we forget, our own faith is founded on texts that speak of wiping out entire pagan tribes, destroying the works of the devil, and binding evil in a pit for a thousand years. It is not enough to disagree or offer a different opinion. The opposition must be crushed. This art has been perfected by the political machines of religious fundamentalism.

It could be that the church is in greater danger from the Trojan horse of religious fundamentalism within its gates than the worldly enemy without.

Kingdom ethics are hard for the church. We are vested in protecting the ways to which we have grown accustomed, rather than being open to change from the in-breaking kingdom of God. Complex ethical issues are easier to address when we "pin the tail" on the enemy from a pulpit, learn the dismissive language of smear, and keep our distance from the one being hung by our tongue until dead. And in so doing, we violate the essence of our faith—God is love. The world turns its back on our worship, younger generations walk out the door in search of a holy conversation, and hardened "saints" miss the chance to grow in the grace and knowledge of our Lord Jesus Christ.

It is time to relearn the spiritual practice of holy conversation. But to relearn it, we must first empty our current arsenal. With caution and grace, I wish to write about the ways we destroy each other in dealing with controversial issues. I know how a few of these demonic weapons work. I have battled with and against them. Others I know because I have seen them full-blooded in the church directory. The local church and the denomination of preference have their arsenal of jihadic weapons. The use of these weapons brings holy conversation to an end. The weapons are named and addressed in the following chapters.

the CRUEL ART OF LABELING

It was not enough to say that John F. Kennedy was Catholic. It had to be added that he would obey Rome rather than do the will of the American people. It was not enough to say that Martin Luther King Jr. wished to overturn the racial injustice of the south. It had to be added that he was a Communist. It was not enough to admit that Dan Quayle could not spell potato. It had to be added that he was not bright enough to be a heartbeat away from the presidency. Political parties perfected the art of labeling.

Once political parties perfected this art, the religious right learned from the best in the business and started creating its own vocabulary of spite: "liberal," "soft on crime," "leftist," "socialist," "tree hugger," "bleeding heart," "tax-and-spend"—you know the list. I'm not suggesting that there are no concerns about those who bear these labels. I'm suggesting that the labels are conversation stoppers. Like the old children's game pin the tail on the donkey, once the donkey is properly pinned, the game is won. If the enemy can be properly labeled or mislabeled, the verdict for destruction is in place. Ready, aim, fire! What follows is not an intelligent, fact-informed, theologically guided discussion on important issues, but a lynching.

This is not new. They called Jesus a friend of sinners, a glutton, and a drunkard. They called him a blasphemer. They suggested that he was somehow a threat to Rome and that anyone who looked the other way would be "no friend of Caesar's." Few of these "labelers" ever had a sit-down face-to-face with Jesus. They just knew he was dangerous. They were right. If his understanding of the world were to prevail, it would turn the world as they knew it upside down.

This is exactly what happened to a visiting woman in Simon's home. The story is recorded in Luke 7:36-50. It is a story ripe with labels. "Sinner" was her label. And it stuck. She might as well have monogrammed her clothes in bright scarlet letters: S-I-N-N-E-R. We are not told whether she was a prostitute, but we suspect it from the way she is spoken about. The label "sinner" separated her from most folks in the community, except the lustful men who wandered into her isolation. They were gone almost as quickly as they came, always taking, never leaving anything behind. If she was the common prostitute of the day, she'd tie up her hair, put a vial of seductive perfume around her neck, and work the streets. People knew what she did.

Simon had a label too. "Host" was his. He was the backbone of the religious community, one who had taken his stance against the pagan culture of Rome. He preferred the way of Torah. We do too. He attended the Promise Keepers rally and defended the integrity of the family. He prayed. He fasted. He tithed. He believed that holiness was the practice of separating from evil of every shape and size. In addition to the label "host," he also wore the label "holy."

Our story is ripe for the perfect clash. The woman enters the home uninvited and approaches Jesus as he reclines on a couch, propped up on his elbow facing Simon. His feet dangle off the end of the couch behind him. The woman stands behind Jesus, wetting his feet with her tears. She loosens her hair, drying the tears with it, and kisses his feet. She splashes perfumed ointment into her hands and begins to massage his feet.

The geography of the room is very important. The woman is behind Jesus, massaging his dangling feet. Jesus faces Simon, who reclines on the couch in front of him. Jesus is sandwiched between *holy host* and *sinner.*

What label will Jesus wear in this story? Until this moment, Luke has introduced Jesus to us as "prophet." But the label is about to be rescinded by Simon. He says of Jesus, "*If this man were a prophet,* he would have known who and what *kind of woman this is* who is touching him—that she is a *sinner*" (v. 39, emphasis added). In other words, Jesus should be able to discern that the foot massage he is getting in Simon's home is not an act of hospitality but a seductive move by a sinful woman. *Prophets* know these things, especially the difference between the holy and the profane.

Before Simon can move to relabel Jesus "not-a-prophet," Jesus speaks. Notice that the woman is still behind Jesus and that Jesus is still facing Simon.

> Jesus spoke up and said to him, "Simon, I have something to say to you." . . . "A certain creditor had two debtors; one owed five hundred denarii, and the other fifty. When they could not pay, he canceled the debts for both of them. Now which of them will love him more?" Simon answered, "I suppose the one for whom he canceled the greater debt." And Jesus said to him, "You have judged rightly" *(vv. 40-43).*

The story suggests that love is empowered by forgiveness. The more deeply we experience forgiveness, the more deeply we love. Jesus interpreted the action of the woman as a response to forgiveness. The tears, the oil, the massage—all have nothing but forgiven gratitude in them. And how did Jesus know this? Well, *prophets* know these things.

Jesus knows the difference between heartfelt worship and dull routine. He knows the difference between obedience and showing off. He knows the difference between a sacrificial gift and a religious tip. He knows the difference between a glittering image and a pure heart. And he doesn't even have to turn around and look. The woman from the story experienced the cancellation of a huge debt and it changed her. Then comes the hinge of the story. Notice again the geography of the room. Jesus swivels. Just as he spoke of the woman to Simon while his back was to her, he now speaks of Simon to the woman with his back toward Simon.

> Then turning toward the woman, he said to Simon, "Do you see this woman? [Jesus is looking straight at her, inviting Simon to do the same.] I entered your house; you gave me no water for my feet, but she has bathed my feet with her tears and dried them with her hair. You gave me no kiss, but from the time I came in she has not stopped kissing my feet. You did not anoint my head with oil, but she has anointed my feet with ointment. Therefore, I tell you, her sins, which were many, have been forgiven; hence she has shown great love. But the one to whom little is forgiven, loves little." Then he said to her, "Your sins are forgiven." But those who were at the table with him began to say among themselves, "Who is this who even forgives sins?" And he said to the woman, "Your faith has saved you; go in peace" *(vv. 44-50).*

Jesus, the *prophet,* now tells what was in Simon's heart without looking. And he declares to the woman that she is forgiven. Labels fly. "Sinner" becomes "forgiven one" and "the one who loves most." At the same time, "holy host" becomes "little forgiven/little love." The world in Simon's home is being turned upside down. This cannot be. So they move to relabel Jesus by asking the question, "Who is this who even forgives sin?" Because if this holy conversation goes further, the woman becomes their sister in the kingdom and they will be forced to deal with her on new terms. It's easier to keep the old labels intact.

It seems to me that somewhere in the world, there should be people who are doing what Jesus did in this story—naming forgiveness and empowering a new identity. As long as conversations occur under the old labels, no one ever changes. As long as we talk about people without ever looking at them, never addressing them, we will be like Simon.

This ploy diverts the conversation from the issue at hand to the persons dealing with the issue. It seeks to tag a person with a label that is dismissive. Rather than a partner in conversation, one becomes a person judged and dismissed as unworthy of consideration. Avoidance is then practiced and conversation never occurs.

If the holy conversation, a generous discourse, is to occur, the labeling must cease. We are not dealing with labels, we are talking to people. Forget their political party and economic status, that they beat you in the last board election, that they are different—and remember that Jesus removes labels. So can we. Then we might be able to talk.

2

PEOPLE *of the* THE LIE[1]

M. Scott Peck authored a book by this title several years ago. Using stories from the Vietnam War and other conflicted events, he made the case that sometimes people can so deceive themselves that they become people of the lie. That is, they actually believe that their version of the story or their characterization of the persons involved is actually true. Reality is reinvented by convenient remembering, convenient forgetting, and careful rationalization. This reality is then reinforced by each retelling of the events in keeping with the more convenient reality. Confirmation by others, often called groupthink, establishes a context and framework for the new interpretation. Time sanctifies it as reality; ritual retellings make it gospel fact.

My wife and I enjoy Broadway musicals. Alongside favorites like *Phantom of the Opera* and *Les Misérables,* we enjoy the musical story *Wicked.* This interesting prequel to the beloved *Wizard of Oz* puts a whole new twist on a well-known story. What if, as the musical *Wicked* suggests, the Wicked Witch was actually a good person who was trying to save Oz? And what if the fates that befell the Lion, the Tin Woodsman, and the Scarecrow were not curses by the Wicked Witch, but her attempt to keep them from being killed by a more sinister curse? And what if Glenda, the Good Witch, was actually a friend of the Wicked Witch and knew the wholesome truth about her but was not courageous enough to confront popular opinion? And what if the Wizard of Oz was actually a fraud, and the father of the Wicked Witch through an adulterous affair?

One of the songs/scripts in *Wicked* occurs in a conversation between the Wizard and his unknown daughter, Elphaba.[2] She later becomes the Wicked Witch through a series of misunderstandings and half-truths. He explains to her how he came to be the leader of Oz. He never asked to be Wizard; the people just needed someone to believe in, someone wonderful. So this "dime a dozen mediocrity" became the Wonderful Wizard of Oz. He posed the idea of a town built of green and postured as their salvation. When challenged with lying, the Wizard said, "Where I'm from, we believe all sorts of things that aren't true. We call it—history."[3] This prompts a proverbial song suggesting that whether a person is a traitor or liberator, a thief or philanthropist, a crusader or invader, depends on which label succeeds.[4]

Once we are given the full history of the characters, the truth swivels in the opposite direction. Suddenly, heroes are villains and villains are heroes. The Munchkins are deceived. Dorothy is journeying toward a false hope. And the celebration of the demise of the witch is actually a moment to be grieved, because the only true and just power in the story is dead.

How do people come to believe lies? And more importantly, how do the people of God become so complicit in them that they actually believe they are defending God?

I grew up in southern Mississippi during the 1960s. The civil rights movement was trying to make inroads into a culture steeped in racial prejudice. I saw oppression firsthand. Most of the white churches had already decided that blacks were not welcome. They had a plan in place should any of "them" try to worship with "us." I heard sermons preached and scriptures quoted defending segregation. But there was one church, a Baptist church on North Locust Street, that opened its arms to anyone who wanted to come. A brave pastor took a minority stance among his clergy peers. He resisted the downward pull of prejudice and welcomed blacks to worship with his white congregation. The KKK burned his church. There was a charred cross on the front lawn. The KKK offered security only to those who sided with them. And most churches did. How did these Christians come to believe this lie?

The church has been wrong many times down through history. Peter was wrong about loading the cultural law of the Jews on the shoulders of the Gentiles. Christians were wrong in their belief that Jerusalem should be taken by crusaders and the enemy occupants killed mercilessly. The Roman Catholic Church was wrong about the scientific discoveries of

Galileo. The Protestant church was wrong about burning martyrs at the stake for positions later embraced as true. The Church of England was wrong to chastise the Wesley brothers, John for preaching in the coal mines and Charles for writing all those worldly tunes. Plenty of preachers have been wrong about end-time scenarios. Christians were wrong to defend slavery and to deny women the right to vote.

It does not surprise me that evil exists in political and economic systems of the world. That is expected. What saddens me is that it exists among the people of God. When God's people believe lies, we are diminished.

Self-deceived religious people may be the most dangerous people in the world, because they are convinced that their cause is of God and their victory endorsed by God. They are not that much different from the Islamic fundamentalists who will blow up their own bodies and kill everyone around them because they believe they are right. Only the self-deceived in the church do not go as far to destroy.

For holy conversation to occur, we must at least be in touch with the reality that we could be wrong. Holy conversation needs an appropriate modesty that is the opposite of arrogance. We can possess a modest opinion about our "foolproofness" and still be deeply convinced of our position. It is a difficult posture, but one that can be given us by the Spirit.

3

ENEMY MAKING

I recently heard someone say, "Nothing unites people like love." I beg to differ. Nothing unites people like the fear of a common enemy. When we are threatened, we mobilize to resist the enemy. It may surprise us what we are willing to do to defend ourselves from a threatening enemy.

Angry religious fundamentalists know this and play on these fears in ways that are irresponsible and damaging to the cause of Christ. Once they have spoken, we are tongue-tied to say anything in opposition lest we be labeled a friend of the enemy.

I saw this happen in March 2010 with the passage of the health care bill. Bricks were thrown through windows, death threats sent to representatives, racial slurs hurled at leaders, and labels like "baby killer" shouted on the floor of the United States Congress. The political tone became tense and mean. Given the partisan divide that exists in our country, I was not too surprised—that is, until I began to hear people of faith pick up the same rhetoric.

This happened in the Lenten season. I was reading Luke's account of Jesus' journey to the cross and was prompted to write a blog titled "Calling Down Fire from Heaven on the Health Care Bill."

> As Jesus was making his way to Jerusalem, he went through Samaria. The Luke account is intriguing. In Luke 9:21-27, Jesus speaks of his appointment with death in Jerusalem, the first of three speeches about betrayal, suffering, and death. The second occurs in Luke 9:43*b*-45. Then, sandwiched between the second and third "death announcements," Luke records three Samaritan encounters. The Jews viewed Samaria as the home of their half-bred, black sheep, theologically inept, rejected cousins. In Luke 9:51-56, Jesus intentionally goes

through Samaria en route to the cross of Jerusalem. The Samaritans do not receive him. I'm guessing this fact means he can't stay in their hotels or eat in their restaurants. No hospitality.

I think it means something that Jesus travels to a place where he is neither wanted nor welcomed en route to the cross. God is always going where rejection is ripe.

The response of the disciples is to command fire to come down from heaven and consume them. Jesus rebukes them for thinking this way. In other words, the disciples of Jesus are not to call down fire from heaven on those they disagree with.

But Luke does not stop here. He mentions two more Samaritans before concluding Jesus' journey to Jerusalem. The second Samaritan story makes a hero of the one who stops to help the man beaten and left for dead along the road (Luke 10:30ff.). The third Samaritan story is about ten lepers healed by Jesus. Only one of them returned to give thanks. And Luke's pregnant pause identifies him: "And he was a Samaritan" (Luke 17:16). Shortly after this third Samaritan story comes the third foretelling of death in Jerusalem (Luke 18:31-34).

I'm reading these texts in the aftermath of the weekend passage of the Health Care Bill. It appears, from what I see, that most Christians are taking their cues from Fox News, Glenn Beck, Rush Limbaugh, and others—and calling down fire from heaven. There is a check in my spirit about this. Yes, I have problems with the lack of careful funding for the program. Yes, I would prefer to see a statute regarding abortion rather than an executive order. Yes, I'd like to see tort reform as part of the legislation to fix health care. The bill is not perfect. But before we call down fire from heaven, maybe we need to see if something good has come out of Samaria.

As president of a university, I've seen graduates, just getting their economic feet under them, looking for their first job in a tight economy, trying to make ends meet. For them to be able to remain on their parents' plan for a few more years (until age 26 in the plan) is nothing short of a blessing to young adults who otherwise would have no insurance. I know a young family whose son is denied health insurance because of a preexisting condition. The child will be able to receive coverage under the new plan. I have a friend who was dropped for insurance coverage because he has a serious disease. This will no longer be done. My parents, who live off their social security check, will get some help with their prescriptions. Thirty-two million people who have no health care today will have it. I can't be dropped because I once took a prescription for arthritis that was also a drug for cancer. Community health centers will receive aid to help the sick. Those who make more than $200,000 to $250,000 a year will kick in more taxes to help fund this. Insurance companies can't operate without regard for the powerless.

As Christians, we have every right to oppose a bill. And fiscal irresponsibility is a good reason to do so. But when we oppose this help being offered to real people, do we sound like modern-day disciples who wish to call down fire from heaven on health care supporters? Should we temper our language to reflect thanksgiving for the benefits that many needy people will receive? Should we carefully state what bothers us about the bill and what we would gladly support? I think it is up for grabs whether Jesus would have voted for or against it. Thirty-two million people without health care would have mattered as much to him as Samaria did.

Now, am I stupid? Do I not know that wrath is coming my way from people who hate Democrats (I'm a registered Republican), Obama (I voted for McCain), and the Health Care Bill (I don't know how I would have voted)? And am I less than a bold follower of Jesus because I hesitate to write about something that God impressed on me—just because angry people will attack? I'm sad that I am afraid to share my heart for fear of the kinds of things people might say. But then, we are called to die with Christ and to entrust our resurrection to him. Maybe the hardest death is to popular opinion, and the hardest place to stand is with those who have no one else standing with them—like the Samaritans.

These issues are good ones to face during the Lenten season as Jesus makes his way to the cross. He went out of his way for those rejected by mainstream Jewish religion, and then he died for all. Following Jesus may not be a popular thing to do.[1]

What is our responsibility as Christians in a culture where enemies are being made by inflammatory rhetoric? When the tail is being pinned on the donkey, dare we wince? When the steamroller of popular opinion is flattening all who take the other side, or even seek a moderate position, do we dare stand in the way? It is far easier to join the attacking army than raise a thoughtful question.

Do we wish to become complicit in the damage done by enemy making? While we would never toss a brick through a window or pose a death threat, can we be sure that those we incite to fear and hatred won't? When we make an enemy, we are responsible to deal with that enemy in ways that honor God.

In our opposition to abortion, have we left room for Christians to rationalize the bombing of abortion clinics or the murder of doctors who perform abortions? I hear a loud "No." But given the immaturity and instability of many within earshot of the church, can we admit our responsibility to use careful language when taking our stance for life? We are our brother's keeper.

When we declare someone an enemy, we unleash something in that person's direction for which we become responsible. In the vernacular of the Old Testament we "curse" the person. A curse was *words spoken with power to do harm*. It was the exact opposite of a blessing—*words spoken with power to do good*. By cursing the enemy, we unleash upon him or her the wish for harm to be done, not the desire for good.

This is not the way of Jesus. When one of his closest followers brandished a sword and whacked off an ear, Jesus quickly moved to heal the wound, not justify it. Peter knew an enemy when he saw one, but Jesus dismissed this kind of violent reaction.

If our tactic is enemy making, we had better know what we are getting ourselves into. We are speaking words that have harm implanted in them, and while we may be able to discipline our response toward the enemy, those who hear us may not. We participate in corporate evil, which needs accusers, judges, and executioners to do its deadly work. We cannot hold the coats of the executioners without getting blood on our own hands.

4

GRANDSTANDING

Similar to enemy making, this ploy reminds people of their fear while reassuring them that the one using this tactic is their savior from this fear. It makes speeches that appeal to the lowest common denominator in the crowd—our joint fear. It repeats time-tested clichés. It casts doubts about anything "new" because the "old" is always more dependable. It is closed to new viewpoints from the outside. It sweeps issues under the rug with generalizations. It seeks to appear conservative while actually being more in keeping with the ways of the world. It postures itself as the safe position. It even quotes Scripture.

This may be the bad yeast that has gotten into the pulpit of our day. If a pastor wants to solidify support, grandstanding is the surest route to popular acclaim. Just tell the congregation members exactly what they want to hear, relieve their fears, castigate all dissenting opinions, and secure them in a religious bubble. Salary increases will certainly follow.

Many preachers have become anything but prophets cut from the cloth of the Old Testament. Isaiah called out the greedy practices of the rich. Amos recited the list of national wrongs topped off by those of his own government. Hosea likened the relationship between God and his people to sexual infidelity. These men spoke truth, as did godly women of courage. They brought as much affliction to the comforted as comfort to the afflicted. They disturbed the peace. They unsettled their congregations. They challenged the status quo.

I've often mused at the call to worship that John the Baptist might have given on a Sunday morning. (See Matt. 3:7-10 for the original version.)

"You brood of vipers, you slithering snakes, what kind of insider information did you get about the coming judgment of God that brings you here today? Buckle your seatbelts, because when God is done running his sword through your lifestyle, you won't even recognize each other. And lest you think you are important to this church, God can make a better church out of the drunks at the local tavern. You'd better straighten up or you are toast. Now let's all turn in our hymnals and sing 'There's a Wideness in God's Mercy.' Stand. Now!"

I'm guessing there would be a board meeting that afternoon and Pastor John would be packing by Monday.

We have endured a generation of seeker preaching that has left us with a gospel less than honest. While the seeker movement taught us to converse with the current context, it may have declawed the gospel's estimation of that context. There is a way to speak the truth in love, treating people with respect. But if being liked is the goal of the preacher, the speech is more likely to be grandstanding than world-shaking.

Having served as a pastor for most of my adult life, I am well aware that people approach the church as consumers. They consume worship, sermons, youth programs, crisis care, and so on. They are even willing to concede that they should drop something in the plate for the consumed goods, probably not 10 percent, but something. It is a transaction:

- "You keep my teenagers busy and out of trouble, and I'll help you buy a van to haul them around."
- "You teach my children some memory verses and put them in a Christmas musical, and I'll help you out with your holy work."
- "You give me an entertaining sermon, and I'll show up as often as it is convenient."
- "You do Mom's funeral, and I'll tip extra next week."

I understand how this works. And congregations are being built today on delivering these goods better than the church down the street—and making sure church is fun.

I listened to a megachurch pastor on TV. He owns the airwaves, sells books, and packs civic centers. He tells people what they already believe, confirming their best intentions. God was not mentioned in the sermon, but seven stories about his own family were. His latest book was being promoted at the bottom of the screen every thirty seconds. People laughed a lot. No one could have been offended by anything he said. It was like a kind cajoling for us all to do better. And it packs the pews, which says more about us than him. We prefer a church without prophets. (Lest I be judged guilty of enemy making, I actually prayed that God would use the broadcast to help someone.)

We all want to be liked. We want people to go home happy. To relieve our discomfort with the poor, we make a big deal about the turkeys at Thanksgiving. Token deeds for the poor. And we never have to talk about our checkbooks and world hunger. To avoid the issue of homosexuality, we select the worst poster child of the gay lifestyle and attack him in a sermon. Everyone says, "Amen!" and we're done with the homosexuals for a while. To salve the social drinkers, we wink at the issue. We would not want to be judgmental. A holy conversation about abstinence never happens.

Grandstanding is how we keep people like ourselves in the pews and solidify our current worldview. We say what they already believe and affirm it as a community truth. The radical gospel of the kingdom of God never penetrates this protective shield with a new vision of the world.

Grandstanding speeches are like a narcotic that turns off the brain and causes everyone to live happily ever after. We root ourselves in the status quo and yearn for the good old days when this was not an issue. But read the faces of young thinkers in the room. Read the faces of those wrestling with the issue. You'll see pain. You'll see hope draining from them. You'll see resignation to the reality that no one cares enough to think it through. This generation is on the way out the door. They stopped by to see if the church that birthed them might want to have an honest conversation.

5

HALF-TRUTH

We ask it in court. "Do you swear to tell the truth, the whole truth, and nothing but the truth, so help you God?" It's a good question. It intends to leave no wiggle room with the truth.

When we take an event and rearrange its retelling for our own purposes, add motives to the characters involved, and explain what they were doing—we have entered the world of half-truth.

We have a campus TV channel at Trevecca Nazarene University. It is used for campus and community announcements as well as a teaching tool for our communication majors. A guest was on our campus for a drama and noted a TV announcement for a yoga class. The guest wrote me a letter of concern about the practice of yoga and its connection to Hinduism. I replied with thanks for the guest's expression of concern and promised to look into the matter. I also expressed my opinion that yoga is viewed in our culture more as a stretching exercise than a religious act of Hinduism. I even reminded the writer that God's people have often taken elements of other religions and sanctified them for Christian use—Canaanite songs became Jewish psalms, pagan feasts became Christian meals, and so on. Paul even used the idol of the unknown god at Athens to declare the gospel of the living God. But I would check into it. Before I knew it, our school was featured in a blog that reported we were "introducing Trevecca students to pagan religions through required classes in yoga." The ad on our community channel had become, according to the blog, an intentional choice to "paganize students through a required curriculum" on a Christian college campus. People were encouraged to "join the movement to throw bums [like me] out of the church before God comes to judge the church." Wow!

Here are the facts. The ad was a spot that we ran for the nearby retirement towers. They have a lot of people with Parkinson's disease who find yoga exercises to be helpful in their mobility. Trevecca doesn't have a yoga class. The president interviews every prospective faculty member for his or her faith fit with the Christian mission of the university.

Half-truth. Yes, there was an announcement for a yoga class. No, there were no paganizing motives behind it, no Hindu connection, and no harm being done. If anything, elderly people were enjoying some health benefits and making friends in an exercise class. Yet the blog's author was impugning the very mission of a Christian university and suggesting that its president be thrown out of the church.

Half-truth happens in so many ways:

- "Well, I heard they were getting a divorce."
- "Bill isn't very good with money. You don't want to buy from him because his business could go under."
- "He's liberal."

All that is needed is a scrap of truth, reformatted for the context and dropped into the conversation at the opportune moment.

Holy conversation never happens when half-truth is given free reign. No one questions the interpretation or defends the slandered.

One of the most painful seasons of my life occurred over church legislation about alcohol consumption. Our denomination calls our people to a position of total abstinence. You'll be reading about this issue in a few chapters. As a pastor who had conducted multiple membership classes, I had been asked many times about our call to total abstinence from alcohol and the lack of scriptural support for such a call. My service to a Christian university placed me in proximity to students asking, "Why is it wrong to drink?" In addition, my friends in Europe were facing similar questions in a culture where alcohol consumption is commonplace. I began to wonder if there was a better way to address the issue than to attack it by listing biblical texts about drunkenness. Is there not a stronger theological reason to call people to total abstinence?

With the help of a theologian and a biblical scholar, I drafted legislation that would expand our listing of scriptures to include texts emphasizing our concern for others and amended our positional statement to include our responsibility for those affected by alcohol. The intent was to deepen our biblical understanding of a call to total abstinence from alcohol. I do not know the motives of those who wished to take issue with the legislation, but it wasn't long before I was labeled "soft on alcohol," "seeking to change the historic position of the church on alcohol," and "in favor of social drinking." During this season, only one person actually picked up a phone and conversed with me about his concerns with the legislation. However, good friends were telling me what was being said. And it hurt.

Few people get to make their defense in a book (like I am doing here). It still pains me to think what people in my own denomination did to me, without even initiating a conversation. The only reason I share this is that it still happens in churches. When we are afraid to discuss an issue, we villainize those who bring it up for discussion. Half-truth becomes full-blown lie, and motives are assigned to actions.

The practice of holy conversation is the best remedy for healing our sickness. We must talk with, not about, each other. The parties being discussed must be invited to the conversation for clarity, dignity, and truth. All it takes is for some brave soul to say, "Let's get all the people in the same room and have a talk about this."

6

SCRIPTURE QUOTING

Mr. Everett, my air-conditioning opponent, quoted from the Bible that was in his head: "The morning air of the Lord will cool the sanctuary." In his mind, God had said it, he believed it, and that settled it. Others use quotes from more authentic biblical versions as the authoritative word to settle issues. And I do not dismiss the authority of the Scriptures as necessary for holy conversation. The revelation of God in Scripture is second only to the revelation of God in flesh. The Word written and the Word enfleshed bear faithful witness to the ways of God.

But I do not believe that Scripture was meant to be used as a conversation stopper. God seems to invite our questions, our doubts, and our wonderings.

I know that my good Baptist friends believe the issue of women preachers is settled by a few verses of Scripture taken point blank. I will try to enter a holy conversation on the interpretation of these texts later in the book. I know that many seven-literal-day creationists believe the science is settled with the quotation of select Genesis texts. I know that many doom-and-gloom, end-time predictors are sure the earth will melt like a marshmallow in a microwave based on a quoted text of Scripture.

And many of these friends are willing to go no further in the conversation than quoting the texts they have built their case on. God said it, they believe it, and that settles it. For them, maybe, but not for the church. And not for the generation headed for the door.

My concern is that we have diminished God by elevating the Bible. When we fuss and fight about the *authority of the Bible*, our focus is usually on the last part of the phrase—"the Bible." I know what we mean by "the Bible," but what do we mean by "authority of"?

The word "authority," as used in Scripture, does not mean being right or wrong, winning an argument, or proving a point. "Authority" in Scripture has to do with God's power to create, save, forgive, heal, and raise the dead. I am not as interested in defending the literal authority of the Bible as in *believing in and experiencing* the authority of the God who is revealed in the Bible. Authority does not rest in biblical words but in the activity of the God being revealed in and through those words. I know that "the word of God is living and active, sharper than any two-edged sword" (Heb. 4:12), but it is not the words on the page that are authoritative. It is the breath of God upon those words when used to create, save, forgive, heal, and raise the dead.

The Pharisees could quote scripture better than we ever hope to, yet they missed the very life that was in them. As Jesus says in John 5:39-40, "You search the scriptures because you think that in them you have eternal life; and it is they that testify on my behalf. Yet you refuse to come to me to have life." They could end a discussion on Sabbath practices with one verse, yet Jesus corrected them for turning a gift into a burden. They could justify not caring for their elderly parents because the money had been pledged to the temple, yet Jesus chided them for lack of mercy and justice. They were so right they were wrong. In the words of Paul, they were trafficking in dead letters (2 Cor. 3). Even the devil quoted scripture in his attempt to turn Jesus from the kingdom mission of the Father toward a religious sideshow that would have entertained the masses (Matt. 4:1-11).

It may be the height of evil to use God's Word to accomplish what God never intends to do. It is forgery, signing God's name to our opinion. It is taking God's name in vain and usurping God's authority for our own purposes. It comes very near to idolatry—turning God into a thing that we can use as we wish, thus making us the real "god."

When we use the authority of the Scriptures to divide the living body of Christ, and when we declare that the words of the Bible are authoritative—

scientifically in Gen. 1
grammatically, since God could not possibly have mispunctuated a sentence
historically, because God's news team was on the spot
prophetically, because God knew that the grasshoppers of the Revelation would become the helicopters of our modern era—

God must think us silly. We are arguing about words. The critical issue is not the authority of the Bible but *the authority of God who has spoken to us through the Bible.* The biblical meaning of "authority" is not "to prove correct" but "to save."

I think the emphasis on Scripture is backward. When we defend the Bible as a perfected document (scientific worldview of its authors, inerrant historical factuality of its writers, perfected punctuation and spelling of its scribes), believing that we herein defend or drive people to believe in God, I think we have made a tactical error. Those who view Scripture as authoritative in their lives are those who are encountered savingly in the reading of the Bible by the Spirit of God, who not only inspired its writing but also inspires its reading. I am not in favor of dismantling the Bible as done in modernism by historical criticism by way of the scientific method. While historical criticism has its scholarly contribution to make, it is not the basis for determining whether Scripture is authoritative in the church. I actually believe that this proof-method of forming one's theological concept of biblical authority is weaker than the Wesleyan process of interpreting Scripture through the lens of tradition, reason, and experience. God reveals and encounters as the active agent in Scripture, rather than needing to be proven as a passive agent.

I believe that God is pained over the tenor of the discussion between the literalists of seven-day creation theories and the evolutionists of the slow creative-process theories. To prove either one correct is not a saving act. God is not wringing his hands hoping we defend the literal interpretation of Gen. 1. Some believe that Moses sat on a mountain and received direct revelation from God about the sequence of creation. I don't know. I wasn't there. But for them, this belief is authoritative.

What I find more exciting and authoritative is the thought that the people of God were exiled in the pagan land of Babylon, listening to pagan stories about the origin of the universe, and the breath of God spoke through a prophet giving them a different understanding. They hijacked the Babylonian tale of creation and declared God to be the one who, in the beginning, created creation and came to take up residence with us in the cosmic temple. Now that's authority—a God who speaks a world-altering word to humans and causes them to reject the prevailing worldview in favor of one in which God is the source and sustainer of all life. God saved them from believing that he was not the Creator. What pagans were crediting to Baal and his buddies, the Israelites credited to

God. The Scriptures have authority in our life when we are changed by the God who is speaking to us in them.

The Revelation of Jesus to John has become the fodder of end-time scenarios. Many have declared this last book of the Bible to be the authoritative guide to deciphering the Antichrist, the mark of the beast, and the details of Armageddon. But what if the writer was not morphing into our century but rather helping a struggling church deal with the monstrous power of Rome? What if there are no futuristic clues about living personalities? What if the end of time cannot be predicted by a numerical exegesis of the Revelation? Does it lose its authority? No. Not if it is read by powerless people struggling with worldly empires that squeeze the life out of them. And not if God speaks to them about the way of a suffering Lamb who is raised to life and becomes the one who holds the future in his hands. And not if they are emboldened by these words and this Spirit to resist the powers in the name of Jesus, in hopes that all things will be made new. If the Revelation forms us to live as hopeful Christians in a dark, pessimistic world, then we have seen the authority of the Scriptures.[1]

When we hold the Sacred Writings, we must know that they are incomplete without holy breath, the Holy Spirit. And this Spirit is in the business of forming us in the likeness of Jesus. This is not to minimize the writings. The Bible is God's revelatory gift to us. It gives us a gathering place for our weekly meetings and a starting place for our daily work. God meets us in the reading of the Scriptures.

Inspired by God, Part 1

All scripture is inspired by God and is useful for teaching, for reproof, for correction, and for training in righteousness, so that everyone who belongs to God may be proficient, equipped for every good work (2 Tim. 3:16-17).

The writers of Scripture were carried along by God, inspired, breathed upon. The primary activity of God was upon the writers, not the pen and ink. God did not guide their hands like a kindergarten teacher forming an *A* on the paper of a compliant beginner. God communicated dynamically with the writers, and they wrote down what they understood—in their own words, in their own time, in the clothing and custom of their culture, reflective of their own personality, stamped by prevalent literary styles, and shaped by their limited understanding of the scientific and historic world. The writers were not court reporters, transcriptionists, or stenographers. They were real humans who experienced the living, breathing God. As they were carried along by the Spirit, they wrote.

This God, who speaks, reveals his creativity through his writing creatures. The Bible is written in different languages, across seven different cultures, over a thousand years, by dozens of authors. It is prose and poetry, stories and letters, songs and riddles, law and history, chronicle and biography, sermon and oracle, proverb and parable. It is a library of sixty-six books. Some of the writers soar in elegance. Others are cumbersome with words. Some would have been best sellers today; others, object lessons in bad syntax. These writing creatures of God are very, very human.

If it was necessary for God to obliterate the "humanness" of the writers to create a perfect manuscript—perfect in scientific theory, chronological history, and linguistic technique—then we must ask questions about several other doctrines. Incarnation—does God need to obliterate the humanity of Jesus to make him fully God? Sanctification—does God obliterate our humanity to make us temples of the Holy Spirit? Must God overpower our limited scientific understanding to reveal himself through us? And what does this thinking do to biblical covenant, the partnership between holy God and fragile human?

The battle these days centers on the inerrancy of the Bible. Most evangelicals agree that the Scriptures inerrantly reveal the will of God concerning us in all things necessary to our salvation and that doctrine and ethics are to be based on the revelation of the Word. We are *sola scriptura* people. The Bible is infallible in revealing God's saving work to us. But some evangelicals go further and claim that the Bible is also inerrant in matters of science, history, and other fields of knowledge.

Given the history of attack on the Bible, it is easy to see why this defensive position took form. Scripture has been pitted against

- the rationalism of the Enlightenment period
- naturalism (which denied the possibility of miracles)
- historical criticism (which often included philosophical assumptions incompatible with Christianity)
- Schleiermacher's religious experience of the nineteenth century (which made Christianity a generic religious experience rather than a divine revelation)
- Huxley's secular humanism
- Freud's behaviorism

- Marx's economic determinism, which redefines the human being
- interpretations of Darwin's theory that were rooted in atheism

When the Bible is attacked from all these directions, it is easy to build a wall and declare the text to be perfect in every way.

Tom Noble[2] reviews the following positions on Scripture:

1. Fundamentalism. This [grassroots] position is a post-World War I movement that rests on the doctrine of the inerrancy of the Bible. It is drawn from [nineteenth-century] Calvinism and declares the Bible not only inerrant on salvation but [also] on all matters of science and history. It rejects higher criticism of Scripture (using historical methods of inquiry to study Scripture in its original context) and hermeneutics (the work of interpreting the Scriptures). Fundamentalism opposes evolution and thereby develops its own scientific theory called creationism. It must then reject all modern science as a means of knowing and understanding the world. The logic of this way of thinking eventually leads to dispensationalism, a way of viewing the future as predetermined from the beginning. For this reason, texts like Revelation are thought to contain clues to the future and predictions of what will unfold in the end times.
2. Mainstream Evangelicalism. This broad coalition of Anglicans, Methodists, Calvinists, Wesleyans, Baptists, Lutherans, Presbyterians, and many others traces its roots to the Protestant Reformation and the [eighteenth-century] Wesleyan revival. All agree on the final authority of the Bible for faith and practice. Evangelicals agree on the validity of historical criticism as long as it is not saddled with the philosophy of naturalism, which rejects the possibility of miracles. Evangelicals also agree that the Scriptures are to be interpreted for the church (hermeneutics) through the acts of preaching and teaching. Evangelicals believe that biblical Christianity is compatible with modern science, not diametrically opposed to it. There is, however, a divide in the Evangelical position on the issue of inerrancy.
   - Those who believe the Bible inerrant on history and science as well as doctrine and ethics are rooted in a Reformed logic that is strongly apologetic. In this view, faith is based on belief in Scripture and an inerrant Bible is necessary for one to come to faith. Faith is highly propositional.

- Those who prefer to view the Bible as inerrant (or the better word might be infallible) on doctrine and ethics are rooted in a different logic, less propositional, more relational. They believe biblical history can be shown to be substantially accurate but are not bothered by minor discrepancies that are attributed to the limited knowledge of the biblical writers. Salvation is primarily "in Christ" as personal response to grace through faith, rather than belief in scriptural propositions—though this is implied in faith as it forms. This position is typical of Anglicans, Wesleyans (Methodists, Nazarenes, etc.), InterVarsity Press, Fuller Theological Seminary, and most European scholars.

The beauty of the Wesleyan position is that Scripture is to be interpreted by use of time-honored doctrinal tradition, reason, and human experience. We study the Bible through the lens of what the church has believed down across centuries, using the reason that God has made us capable of through education in scientific and historical methods, and by listening to the experiences of humans as they have interacted with God. In this way the church not only interprets Scripture but also formulates doctrine.

The sad reality is that many people are more influenced by popular fundamentalist preachers than by their own rich theological traditions. Fear has seized them as clichés have replaced strong theology. The Word of God has become a battlefield rather than a gift of God. Those who use the Bible to bash others are violating their own logic. They usurp the Bible to support their interpretation, while attacking those who interpret the Bible any other way.

If the Scriptures are just words on a page, they become dangerous when used without regard for the Father they reveal, the Son they narrate, and the Spirit who gives them breath.

> In Herman Melville's novel *White Jacket* one of the sailors takes sick with severe stomach pains. Dr. Cuticle, the ship's surgeon, is delighted to have a patient with something more challenging to his art than blisters. He diagnoses appendicitis. Several shipmates are impressed into nursing service. The deckhand is laid out on the operating table and prepared for surgery. Dr. Cuticle goes at his work with verve and skill. He makes his cuts with precision, and, on the way to excising the diseased organ, points out interesting anatomical details to the attendants around the table, who had never before seen the interior

of an abdomen. He is absorbed in his work, and obviously good at it. All in all it is an impressive performance, but the sailor attendants are, to a man, not impressed but appalled. The poor patient, by the time he has been sewn up, has been a long time dead on the table. Dr. Cuticle, enthusiastic in his surgery, hadn't noticed. The sailors, shy in their subservience, didn't tell him.[3]

All too easily, what began as living breath becomes as dead as a cadaver. We are left to poke, probe, dissect, analyze, and autopsy. And like Dr. Cuticle, many of us were never aware of the moment when the breathing stopped. We're in the middle of a discussion and we need to prove a point, so we reach for the scalpel of Scripture and slice open the opponent with a choice quote. Life has left the conversation because we no longer pay attention to the breath of God in Scripture. This is deadly.

Inspired by God, Part 2

All scripture is inspired by God and is useful for teaching, for reproof, for correction, and for training in righteousness, so that everyone who belongs to God may be proficient, equipped for every good work (2 Tim. 3:16-17).

The Spirit of God is just as involved in the inspiration of readers/listeners as in the inspiration of the writers. We are supernaturally assisted by God in the act of reading Scripture. When young Timothy's community opened the scrolls and read ancient words, God breathed upon them and they became the people of God, taught by God, rebuked and corrected by God. They became story-shaped people. And the breath of God formed Christ in them.

I am a fan of *Star Trek.* I began watching in the early days of Captain Kirk, Scotty, and Mr. Spock. The USS *Enterprise* was equipped with technology that allowed them to scan another vessel. By scanning, they could gain important information—life signs, weapons powering up, where to beam. The early *Enterprise* was a master at collecting information from another vessel without being detected. In this way, it held the upper hand.

That's how we learn to read. We scan the printed material in front of us. We collect the information we wish to use to better ourselves. We conquer the material for an exam. We cut and paste the material for a presentation. We quote and notate to make a point. We argue to prove our opinion better. When we read, our sitting position is suggestive of our power. The printed words are beneath our all-seeing eyes. We read down. We are in the position of power over the words, and we believe we can make them serve our interests. That's how the currency of information works in our world. Reading the Bible this way turns it into a crossword puzzle to solve, a lock to pick, a wilderness map to study, information to absorb, a weapon for attack.

The latest version of the USS *Enterprise* has a different technology. Captain Jean-Luc Picard knows when his vessel is being scanned by another. On any ordinary day in space, he becomes aware that life other than his own is looking into him, discerning and knowing him. This is the capacity that we need, the capacity to know that we are being scanned by a loving God who wishes to save us in every way. Maybe it is better to be known by God than to know self-selected information. Maybe when we read the Scriptures, we are the ones being read.

Holy conversation gathers people around the Scriptures with the intent of listening to them and being shaped by them. Exploration of Scripture takes us deeper into God and deeper into community.

7

CHARACTER ASSOCIATION

My first car was a red Volkswagen Beetle. My cousin and I co-owned it. The carburetor did not function correctly, and one of us had to sit in the back with the seat removed and work the choke. The engine was in the trunk. We drove the "under repair" vehicle in our backyard, round and round and round, until we were old enough to get a driver's license. By the time we hit the road, the grass in our backyard had an Indy track dug into it. We had also repaired the carburetor, making a backseat accelerator unnecessary. The little VW was a tough, durable car. I still see them on the road today. And every time my wife sees one, I get punched.

The game was called Punch Buggy. Spotting a VW gave you permission to slug the arm of the person you were with. I much preferred the other VW spotting game—Perdiddle. In this game, if you saw a VW with only one working headlight, you had permission to kiss your date. A VW today can get you kissed or punched. You're never quite sure which one to expect.

The "gotcha" games of our childhood and youth have made their way into the jihadic tactics of the church. When an enemy is named and you are associated with this enemy in any way, you automatically get punched. It is a reflexive response that is unthinking. Similar to Pavlov's dog, the stimulus of the association causes a reaction.

Side with a bill sponsored by a liberal Democrat, and you must be "one of them." Side with a bill sponsored by an ultraconservative Republican, and you are "one of those." Read a quote from Thomas Merton or Brian McLaren, and you now believe everything Catholic or you are a full-blown supporter of everything emergent. Print a book of testimonials from postmodernists, and be prepared to be named an enemy of all that is traditional. Assign a controversial book as reading material in a college class, and be prepared to defend everything ever written by the author as if it is your own thought. Invite someone to speak on your campus who holds a different perspective, and get ready for the negative mail.

This is nothing new. In the McCarthy era, the enemy was Communism. Anyone who did not meet the expectations of those in power was dismissed by being called a Communist. And if the so-called Communist had ever checked a book on socialism out of the local library, that was all the proof needed.

I know this sounds silly. And it is. About as silly as believing you have the right to punch someone because a VW drove by.

Educated Christians are well-read people (like those of you who are taking the time to read this book). And it is not uncommon for believers to read books from differing perspectives. This is how we become critical thinkers and learn to make our case in the world. A college student would be considered uneducated if he or she had never read Hitler or studied the philosophical assumptions of atheism. A missionary to a Muslim country would be foolish to enter a culture without understanding the history and culture of Islam. A social worker would be unprepared to work with a family of violence without reading case studies of brutality and abuse. Are these things Christian? No. Is it wrong to read these authors and study these topics? No.

The issue is not whether one's character is to be assumed by the authors he or she reads or the topics he or she studies. The greater issue is the reason a person reads and studies and the conclusions drawn from this. I remember as a pastor having several students tell me that the Bible was wrong about homosexuality. They had read "reputable Greek scholars" and reached different conclusions. So I asked them what they were reading. I bought their recommended authors and joined them with their hero books in one hand and the Bible in the other. We read their books together. I was able to guide them to understand the controlling agenda of their authors and how far off base they were in the scriptural interpretations they were proposing.

I've read books I don't agree with to understand the logic of a dangerous movement or philosophy. I've gone to hear speakers I disagree with to determine how they work their black magic on crowds. I've even listened to popular music I don't like so I can converse with a younger generation about the values being promoted in their top ten songs.

Banning authors, speakers, books, music, and topics is not the way of God's people in the world. And assassinating the character of those who dare to know about these is even worse. It suggests that we are afraid to stand toe-to-toe with people who think differently. It sends us running into the walled church where we only speak with those who already agree with us. When we take a closed, defensive posture toward "those people out there," it piques the curiosity of our youth to explore them on their own. As with sex and alcohol, they are drawn to the mystery of things we won't talk about.

While it is important to guide the education of our children and to watch over their reading material and education, it is also important to prepare our youth to stand on their own two feet in the world. Our Christian colleges are one of the best places in the world for a frank discussion of authors, value systems, philosophies, and differing worldviews. The only place better is the home where parents begin to talk with their teens about authors, political movements, ethical matters, and controversial issues.

The day a church, a college, or a Christian shies away from reading a controversial author out of fear of being associated with the character of the author will be a sad day indeed. If enemy authors are named and if you are caught reading them, quoting from them, assigning them as a class reading requirement, or inviting them to speak, the opposition will have permission to punch you.

I'd rather kiss the folks who dare to understand the world we live in.

section 2

THE ISSUES THAT DIVIDE US

The following chapters deal with seven issues that are causing division in the body of Christ today:

Women in the Biblical Church
Religion and Politics
Alcohol
Human Sexuality
Homosexuality
Science and Religion
The Emerging Church

This list is not exhaustive. Actually, it barely scratches the surface. Having served as a pastor, I am well aware that division can occur over youth pastors, carpet colors, and multiple family members serving on the church board. However, these seven specific issues seem to be the places where the church meets the world and conversation is most needed. Quiet prejudices are forming around these issues, and younger generations are puzzled by the lack of clarity coming from the church.

I am prejudiced. It will become apparent where I stand on most of the issues addressed. And it is my hope to influence thought on these issues. To suggest that I can find total neutrality on these issues is to overestimate human capacity. However, my prayer is that the tone and spirit will enlighten rather than divide Christians. My prediction is that readers may wholeheartedly agree with me in one chapter and find themselves diametrically opposed in the next. And the reader may be right. I am still growing in understanding the Scriptures, and my reasoning powers are far from perfect. However, I bear witness that the Spirit of God is moving me toward love rather than division as the way the world will know that we are Christians.

8

WOMEN *in the* BIBLICAL CHURCH

Is it a man's world? If you surveyed the leadership level of this country's institutions—school boards, colleges, political parties, businesses, banks, executive boards, churches—men would dominate. Does this say something about male superiority or about culture or about God's created order or about the curse of sin?

Women's issues in America have a long history—education, the right to vote, equal pay, protection under the law from domestic violence, double standards in sexual behavior, economic exploitation, Title IX sports issues, political office, glass ceilings in corporate businesses, sexual discrimination, sexual harassment, priesthood, ministry, and military. Lots of issues. And if you travel to other places in the world, the list gets longer: the right to go out in public, to show her face, to speak to a man, to learn to read, sterilization, the murder of female babies, rape, slavery, and forced prostitution. The way of women in this world has not been easy.

The apostle Paul wrote, "For all of you who were baptized into Christ have clothed yourselves with Christ. There is neither Jew nor Greek, slave nor free, male nor female, for you are all one in Christ Jesus" (Gal. 3:27-28, NIV). When we are baptized into Christ, a new creation is born, a people whose acceptance is not based on culture, gender, or economic status. The church is God's signal to the world of the new creation in Jesus. It is nothing less than the presence of the resurrected Christ making all things new through sanctification by the Spirit.

But the church has often sent a very different signal to the world. When we model male dominance, we are not the church of Gal. 3:27-28. We are worldly.

Even as I write these words, I hear the protest rising from some quarters of Christianity. It is true that when we examine the New Testament, we find biblical texts that, taken at face value, make it appear that God intended men to rule. All of these texts appeal to the creation accounts of Genesis.

So let's begin in the beginning and have a holy conversation.

The cultural world at the time of the writing of Genesis was a male-dominated universe. Female submission was assumed. It was a cultural reality. Because of this, the purpose of the creation accounts had little to do with defining gender roles. These stories in the first three chapters of Genesis are about a radical understanding of the God of the Jews—a God who is revealed as a covenant-making Creator. When we come to these texts, we expect them to reflect a male-dominated viewpoint. Yet in reality what we find are some radical claims being made. Let's take a look.

> So God created humankind in his image, in the image of God he created them; male and female he created them. God blessed them, and God said to them, "Be fruitful and multiply, and fill the earth and subdue it; and have dominion over the fish of the sea and over the birds of the air and over every living thing that moves upon the earth" *(Gen. 1:27-28).*

We see human defined as being both male and female, and the command to subdue and to have dominion over all of creation is given not just to male but also to female.

> Then the LORD God said, "It is not good that the man should be alone; I will make him a helper as his partner." . . . So the LORD God caused a deep sleep to fall upon the man, and he slept; then he took one of his ribs and closed up its place with flesh. And the rib that the LORD God had taken from the man he made into a woman and brought her to the man. Then the man said, "This at last is bone of my bones and flesh of my flesh; this one shall be called Woman, for out of Man this one was taken." Therefore a man leaves his father and his mother and clings to his wife, and they become one flesh. And the man and his wife were both naked, and were not ashamed *(2:18, 21-25).*

God creates a "helper" for the man. This word appears twenty-one times in the Old Testament, and in nine of these God is being called "the helper." A helper is one whose help is indispensable or one who comes to rescue. The word "helper" is never used to mean a mere assistant or a subservient person.

In these two creation texts there is no hint of domination of the male over the female. And yet we see that people continue to try to read just that into the text. Some have said that the creation order suggests superiority—the male first, the female later. But if that is the case, man is inferior to plants, animals, and insects.

What we do see in Genesis is man and woman jointly reflecting the image of God, man and woman jointly caring for God's creation, and man and woman jointly commissioned by God to rule and take dominion.

Does all of this mean there is no hint of male dominance in the creation account? No. Genesis 3:16 says, "To the woman he said, 'I will greatly increase your pains in childbearing; with pain you will give birth to children. Your desire will be for your husband, and he will rule over you'" (NIV). This dark moment in the story occurs only after the creatures have sinned. It is in the list of curses that accompany sin. The serpent is cursed to crawl, the woman is cursed to bear children with pain and to be ruled by men, and the man is cursed to hard, sweaty labor. God is saying to the woman that the consequence of sin, the curse of sin, is that she will be ruled by men. The woman will desire a husband, but the husband will desire to rule. She wants a mate, but he wants to be master. She wants a lover, but he wants to be lord. This, according to Gen. 3, is the curse of sin. And human history is proof that Gen. 3 is true: snakes crawl, women labor in childbirth, men rule, and work is hard. The future looks bleak for women.

Fast-forward in time, when God became flesh among us. The ministry of Jesus was a social revolution. He offered inclusion in God's kingdom to all—the poor, the sick, the social outcast, the Gentile, the slave, the marginalized, the rejected. All were invited into the kingdom and given equal status.

This was liberating news to women. He taught them; they followed him. He talked to them; they became his disciples. He touched them; they were healed. They often showed deeper insight and more courage than men. They were first at the cradle and last at the cross. They were the messengers of the resurrection. Without question, Jesus parted with social custom and bridged the gender gap by his inclusion of women in the work of the kingdom. You do not hear a hint of male superiority in the gospel accounts of Jesus' dealings with women. And as the resurrected Jesus ascends to heaven in Acts 2, the Holy Spirit is poured out upon the followers of Jesus, both male and female. Women were in the upper room with the men, preaching and prophesying. The Spirit is poured out on sons and daughters.

So what do we do with the pesky New Testament texts about women being silent, men being the heads of their wives, and wives being submissive? Some scholars paint Paul as a chauvinist and say that this was his problem, thus excusing these texts. Yet it was Paul who says that in Christ "there is no longer male and female; for all . . . are one" (Gal. 3:28). Paul also encouraged women in leadership and teaching roles. And when Paul writes about the gifts of the Spirit given for service, he does not make the gifts gender specific. So what's going on in the troublesome texts that we find?

This is where an impasse occurs for fundamentalists. If your way of viewing scripture forbids interpreting the Scriptures through biblical hermeneutics or the use of historical methods to study the Bible, the conversation ends here. The literal word is taken at face value without regard for the culture, the historical context, the understanding of the author, or the belief that the Spirit can speak through the preached word to current situations today. You will not bring reason, human experience, or doctrinal traditions to the task of interpreting these texts. If this is your position, what follows will make little sense to you. But if you believe that the Spirit of God can work through godly people to speak fresh words to situations that didn't even exist in the first century, then you may wish to read on.

Let's take a closer look at these troublesome texts.

Imaging Christianity in Corinth

> I commend you because you remember me in everything and maintain the traditions just as I handed them on to you. But I want you to understand that Christ is the head of every man, and the husband is the head of his wife, and God is the head of Christ. Any man who prays or prophesies with something on his head disgraces his head, but any woman who prays or prophesies with her head unveiled disgraces her head—it is one and the same thing as having her head shaved. For if a woman will not veil herself, then she should cut off her hair; but if it is disgraceful for a woman to have her hair cut off or to be shaved, she should wear a veil. For a man ought not to have his head veiled, since he

is the image and reflection of God; but woman is the reflection of man. Indeed, man was not made from woman, but woman from man. Neither was man created for the sake of woman, but woman for the sake of man. For this reason a woman ought to have a symbol of authority on her head, because of the angels. Nevertheless, in the Lord woman is not independent of man or man independent of woman. For just as woman came from man, so man comes through woman; but all things come from God. Judge for yourselves: is it proper for a woman to pray to God with her head unveiled? Does not nature itself teach you that if a man wears long hair, it is degrading to him, but if a woman has long hair, it is her glory? For her hair is given to her for a covering. But if anyone is disposed to be contentious—we have no such custom, nor do the churches of God *(1 Cor. 11:2-16).*

The issue in this passage is not male control of women but how a woman's hair or uncovered head affected the understanding of Christianity in Corinth. Apparently, some of the women were bucking culture and letting their hair hang loose, just like the pagan priestesses who went into a prophetic frenzy at the local pagan temple. And they were also shaving their heads, reminiscent of the hairstyle of the city prostitutes. Whether pagan or prostitute, the hairstyles of these women sent a damaging signal to the people of Corinth about the nature of Christianity. So Paul is asking them to honor their husbands by not representing themselves in the style of the pagans or prostitutes. In Corinthian culture, husbands had power to dominate their wives. But Paul appeals, not to the husband, but to the wife, to view her behavior in the light of the gospel. He calls for mutual respect: "In the Lord woman is not independent of man or man independent of woman." Paul calls for mutual regard for each other, and he asks the husbands and wives to work out this problem without being contentious.

How Christians Worship

God is a God not of disorder but of peace. (As in all the churches of the saints, women should be silent in the churches. For they are not permitted to speak, but should be subordinate, as the law also says. If there is anything they desire to know, let them ask their husbands at home. For it is shameful for a woman to speak in church) *(1 Cor. 14:33-35).*

This is a minor comment in a whole chapter that deals with the disruption of worship by those who would stand and speak in unintelligible language. Here, Paul is placing restrictions on this disruptive behavior. His goal, seen in the last words of the chapter (v. 40), is that all things are to be done decently and in order.

Apparently, similar to what we will see in 1 Timothy, the Corinthian women have a tendency to take over the services with their frenzied prophecies. So Paul suggests that they keep quiet and talk with their husbands at home. Paul has already instructed them (chap. 11) to cover their heads so that they can pray and prophesy. Paul is not forbidding their participation in worship but simply calling for an end to their disruptive outbursts.

Paul, the Radical Feminist

> Be subject to one another out of reverence for Christ. Wives, be subject to your husbands as you are to the Lord. For the husband is the head of the wife just as Christ is head of the church, the body of which he is the Savior. Just as the church is subject to Christ, so also wives ought to be, in everything, to their husbands. Husbands, love your wives, just as Christ loved the church and gave himself up for her *(Eph. 5:21-25).*

Paul isn't saying anything radical when he says that the husband is the head of the wife. In the Ephesian culture, it would be like saying "grass is green." These verses feel awkward to us but not to them. To them, this was the same old, same old—nothing new.

What is radical in this passage is Paul's call that husbands and wives submit to each other out of reverence to Christ. The text calls for mutual submission. The husband is called to submit to his wife, to love her as Christ loves the church, to lay down his life for her, to care for her as his own body. This is radical, new, and different. This is akin to announcing that grass is pink. Because of our modern cultural perspective, this sounds like male dominance; but in that culture, this is radical feminism. In a culture cursed by sin, where men ruled, Paul called for a new way of relating rooted in the relationship between Jesus and his bride.

We must read these texts in light of their culture, asking what reality they are pointing toward. These texts imagine equality in Christ between men and women, Spirit-anointed unity, gifts given to each for service, mutual submission and respect, and a joint reflection of the image of God. These texts give us a bright outlook for the place of women, but there is still one more text to look at, and this text is the one most often quoted to forbid women to preach or lead in the church.

The Redemption of Gullible Women

> First of all, then, I urge that supplications, prayers, intercessions, and thanksgivings be made for everyone, for kings and all who are in high positions, so that we may lead a quiet and peaceable life in all godliness and dignity. This is right and is acceptable in the sight of God our Savior, who desires everyone to be saved and to come to the knowledge of the truth. For there is one God; there is also one mediator between God and humankind, Christ Jesus, himself human, who gave himself a ransom for all—this was attested at the right time. For this I was appointed a herald and an apostle (I am telling the truth, I am not lying), a teacher of the Gentiles in faith and truth. I desire, then, that in every place the men should pray, lifting up holy hands without anger or argument; also that the women should dress themselves modestly and decently in suitable clothing, not with their hair braided, or with gold, pearls, or expensive clothes, but with good works, as is proper for women who profess reverence for God. Let a woman learn in silence with full submission. I permit no woman to teach or to have authority over a man; she is to keep silent. For Adam was formed first, then Eve; and Adam was not deceived, but the woman was deceived and became a transgressor. Yet she will be saved through childbearing, provided they continue in faith and love and holiness, with modesty *(1 Tim. 2:1-15).*

The primary issue in 1 and 2 Timothy is false teaching. The Greek word is found thirty-six times in the New Testament, and twenty-four of these are in the letters to Timothy. Timothy is dealing with myths, fables, godless chatter, false doctrine, disputes, and divisive arguments. He is charged with guarding the gospel in the face of false teaching.

The women of Timothy's church were primarily uneducated, as were most of the women in his day. It was definitive of the culture. They had not been trained in Jewish law or in Gentile schools. As a result, women were viewed like Eve before the serpent—gullible. These women had fallen prey to false teaching and were acting and dressing like their pagan priestess counterparts in the local shrines and temples. They were teaching heresy in seductive ways. It was Timothy's intent to find a solution to this problem, and that is the issue being addressed in this text.

In a radical cultural move, the writer commands that women be allowed to learn, that they not remain gullibly uneducated. Instead, they are to be taught and educated in the ways of truth. It says that this is to be "done in silence." We often view this in a negative sense, as if the women in Timothy's church are being told to shut up. But this is actually a complimentary word. To learn in silence means to listen respectfully to those who teach you in faith. Men were called to the same "silence" with their rabbis. And so, the call is for women to be theologically and doctrinally trained by those who know the truth.

We also see in this passage that women were prohibited from teaching, no doubt because they were uneducated and untrained. They were also not to have authority over men. In other literature of the time, the word for authority meant "to murder, to assassinate, or to destroy." Some scholars think that its use here suggests the kind of control the pagan priestesses held over men in the act of temple prostitution. So women who have not been taught the faith are commanded not to teach or to hold sway over men; otherwise, like Eve with Adam, they may lead the men astray by false teaching.

This text, rather than negating the role of women as teachers, actually calls for women to learn so that they won't hurt the church by their teaching.

The church is called to be God's sign to the world of a new creation, a people who have been redeemed from the curse of sin. What does this new creation look like?

- Men and women are partners in caring for creation.
- Sons and daughters can be seen preaching and teaching.
- There is mutual submission between husbands and wives.
- All are allowed to use their spiritual gifts without regard for gender.
- Christian men and women treat and teach each other in ways that are radically new in our culture.

We send this sign by our marriages, which are partnerships of love and respect. We send this sign by our ministries, when men are in the nursery and women are in our pulpits and on our church boards. We send this sign through singles groups where relationships are healthy, where acquisition is not the dominant agenda. We send this sign by the way we dress, the way we talk to each other, by justice in our courts, by equality in the marketplace, by openness at the tables of power, by courtesy and respect in public, and by the absence of flirtatious, harassing, or demeaning behavior toward one another. We send this sign by the presence of Christ that dwells within us and can be sensed by the people around us. The way we treat women is God's sign to the world that all things are being made new in Christ. We are bearing witness of a God who sent forth a Son to redeem us from the curse of sin and to make *all* things new.

9

RELIGION *and* POLITICS[1]

The question is asked many ways. Can faith and politics mix? Can there be a true separation between church and state? Are there two realms—sacred and secular? Is it possible for a Christian to be a Democrat? Is it possible for a Christian to be a Republican? Does it matter to God whether we vote for Obama or McCain?

In the words of John Ortberg, "God is not interested in your spiritual life. God is just interested in your life."[2] The entire creation belongs to God, and he claims it as his own—every realm, every throne, every sovereign inch. The kingdom of God is sovereign over politics. If our faith is not political, it does not embrace all that God is interested in.

God has come down to earth in the person of Jesus and has engaged this world through suffering love. If politics deals with the use of power to help or harm, the well-being of creatures, the care of the earth and its resources, the systems of justice, the peace of the nations—then God is right in the middle of it.

Our faith is not a private matter. It is corporate, communal, and public. To be blunt, God cares about what we eat, who we sleep with, how we spend our money, and the work we do. Faith and politics are inseparable for the engaged, thinking Christian. But we have a problem.

We are dual citizens in time and space. Our first and primary place of belonging is the kingdom of God. This is the realm where God is at work making all things new. In this kingdom, his name is hallowed; his will done. We draw our life in this kingdom from the Spirit of the resurrected Lord, whose ascension to the right hand of the Father assures that all things will be redeemed from death even as was his own body from the grave. We are called to constant alignment with the ways of this God. And our hope is not for victory in heaven by and by but on earth here and now. Ours is no escapist religion that surrenders the created order to the devil and politics but instead a faith that has tasted the beginning of the end of all things in the resurrection of Jesus.

However, we also live in the cultures of the kingdoms of this world. In Paul's language, there is a ruler of the power of the air who lives within those who practice disobedience. There is a corporate evil among us. We are not fully or finally delivered from it. It has wormed its way into our thoughts and actions more deeply than we know. The deception of this hideous evil is that the world belongs to these dark powers.

In the contest between the kingdom of God and the kingdoms of this world, the whole creation is up for grabs. Because Christianity often appears to be trailing ten to two in the bottom of the ninth, we have abandoned our hope for the restoration of all things in favor of being raptured to a place where sin never got a good foothold. Bad move.

Even our songs know it:

And though this world, with devils filled, should threaten to undo us,
We will not fear, for God has willed his truth to triumph through us.[3]

This is my Father's world; the battle is not done.
Jesus who died shall be satisfied,
And earth and heaven be one.[4]

Yes, there are two kingdoms. One is life giving; the other, death inducing. One is God honoring; the other, self-sovereign. One is eternal; the other, fizzling out even as you read. We are called to be invested in the kingdom that is young, fresh, life giving, and en route to us from the future. So we live in this world while not being of this world, which is quite difficult to do.

As followers of God, we are given the capacity to see and hear the guiding activity of God all around us and to participate in it. As the world pressures us in one direction, the Spirit of the kingdom guides us in another. The goal of God is to restore in us the mind of Christ. We are meant, as Christians, to have a Christian worldview. This means that we draw our political understandings from God.

Political arrangements can get messy when we look to our Scriptures, because the people of God have lived under six different forms of governance and none of them have brought the kingdom to earth.

1. We've been slaves in Pharaoh's Egypt. To be without voice, vote, or government representative is horrible. No one gave a rip about our well-being. From this setting, we learned to cry out to God on behalf of the powerless, asking that this enslaving government be brought to its knees before the power of God. Our memory of this time guides our thinking about unborn children (remember the midwives of Exod. 1), the poor, nations without rights, and ethnic cleansing.
2. We've been a loose federation of tribes with no central government. This story is found in Joshua and Judges and happened just after our entrance to the Promised Land. The only time we needed a central government was in crisis or threat, which seems to suggest the less government the better. Republicans tend to favor this one. When trouble came, the Spirit of the Lord would fall on a leader (male or female), and he or she would unify the people to resist the threat as guided by the protective Spirit. Once the enemy was defeated, the people would disband and get back to living as normal. There was no king but God.
3. But soon, we wanted to be like the other nations around us. In a sense, we wished to join the League of Nations. For this, we needed a king. And kings need palaces, armies, taxes, cabinets, courts—well, you know. And there you go—government. God did not want to give us a king, but he finally relented. It is frightening when God gives in to our wishes. This story is found in the books of Samuel, Kings, Chronicles, and Psalms. The form of government was technically a theocracy, but it actually turned out to be a succession of really bad rulers sandwiched between a few good ones. The king was thought to be the God-appointed, priest-anointed son of God sitting on a throne speaking for God. This is God and government hand-in-hand. Sometimes it worked. Most of the time it didn't. While not the Christian kind, this is how fundamentalist Islamic states are run.

4. The failure of this government led to a new political arrangement called exile. We were conquered by the Babylonians and hauled off to Babylon to live out our days under a pagan power. The Babylonians were somewhat merciful but believed in the back of their minds that our God was a pushover. To them, Baal had triumphed over Yahweh, and that's why we were in Babylon. We were not slaves. We were permitted to live as we pleased but were subtly encouraged by all the Baal hoopla to assimilate. Like the Borg on *Star Trek*, resistance would be futile. This story is found in Isaiah, Ezekiel, and other prophetic books. From this arrangement we learned it is a challenge to keep rituals, worship, and sacred memories alive when surrounded by pagans. The role of Christians in this kind of political arrangement is to remember who we are and not forsake our faith. Resistance to the dominant culture can be costly.
5. We have also been a majority in our own land, but under Roman rule. This story is in the Gospels. Jesus lived on earth under this arrangement. The Pharisees refused to assimilate. The Sadducees made concessions to Rome for the privilege of getting along in reasonable peace. The Zealots ran an underground resistance movement. As far as we can tell, Jesus voted for none of the above. His kingdom business seemed to go on in the middle of this; he was fully aware of what was happening but not devoted that passionately to any party.
6. We've been Christian minorities in cities and nations where we are citizens but under suspicion. This story is told in the letters of Paul, the letters to the churches of the New Testament, and the Revelation of Jesus to John. We did missionary work as the first known Christians. Sometimes we were a threat. Sometimes we were welcomed.

So where are we now? We're certainly not slaves. We're definitely not a theocracy. The United Methodist bishops didn't inaugurate George Bush, and the United Church of Christ didn't inaugurate Barack Obama. We're a little like the exiles in Babylon in a pagan culture, but the ruler of our nation is a Christian, so where is home? We may be becoming a minority and needing to learn to live in post-Christian America like the Pharisees. I wonder if that's why the Pharisees, Sadducees, and Zealots are making a comeback in new uniforms. When the church crawled in bed with the Republican party and won the White House, the Senate, and the House, we finally claimed a moral majority, but even then, we didn't transform our culture. We are no longer a majority voting block that can elect our candidate and thereby secure our agenda.

So we are finding our way in the politics of our world as it is today. Stating the obvious, the kingdoms of this world will not embrace the kingdom of God and his righteousness. There may be overlap in the two agendas, but not much. Our ultimate hope is rooted in neither the Republicans nor the Democrats but in Christ, who makes all things new. Do not let any president's hand resting on a swearing-in Bible fool you. Our government is not seeking to align itself with the kingdom of God. Yet being a citizen of God's kingdom is not an excuse to drop out, not vote, and care less. We are called to be light in the darkness, God's persons in this world.

We speak truth to power. The current practice of politics in our world is best described as enemy making. Make everyone afraid of what the other political party will do if elected, huddle the fearful into your party tent, and constantly reinforce the horrible things these people are trying to do to you and your country. If you do this well, you will secure an entire geographical area and can claim it as a red state or a blue state. If you are really successful, you will co-opt the once unbiased news media and will have whole channels devoted to your cause of trashing the other party. Newspapers will also take sides, as well as businesses whose profit making depends on who is in power. And you will win the election and be given the reins for four years.

It's hard to play in this game when, as Christians, our calling is to refuse to make or be an enemy. We love our enemies, turn the other cheek, walk the extra mile, bless them and pray for them and love them just like our Father in heaven loves his enemies. Our business is not enemy making but enemy loving. Our business is not dividing the country into blue and red states, but being a people of one accord. Our business is not securing the power to rule, but doing justice, showing mercy, and walking humbly with our God.

So when it comes to politics, it feels as though we are fighting with both hands tied behind our back.

I see good and bad in both political parties. The Republicans seem to lean into the Wisdom Literature best—personal responsibility, a work ethic, just rewards, good decisions, wise rulers. The Democrats live closer to the Prophets—care for the downtrodden, the rich helping the poor, justice for the powerless at the city gate, not going to war.

I suppose when it comes to voting, these are the questions Christians ought to be asking:

1. Under which leader is the world most likely to be at peace?
2. Under which leader will the people of God have the most freedom to carry out the agenda of the kingdom of God?
3. Under which leader will human life be protected, valued, and nourished?
4. Under which leader will justice be carried out in creating a peaceful society of neighborly concern?
5. Under which leader will I be expected to be a more responsible citizen in my community rather than a dependent consumer of government goods?
6. Under which leader will honorable work be valued and made available for all to participate in?
7. Under which leader will fragile persons be given the aid they need to become whole again and then be expected to live as responsible citizens?

I recall a Sunday during the previous presidential election. We had been having discussions with a local political party who wanted to distribute voter guides to our congregation. Their voter guides claimed to be neutral, simply asking questions of concern for Christians and showing how the candidates had voted. In reading through the guides, I found them to be anything but neutral. The political agenda was obvious, and the issues severely shortsighted and narrow. The goal of the voter guide was to support the candidates of one party while de-Christianizing the candidates of the opposing party. I finally settled the issue by telling them that we had our own "voter guides" and would be distributing them on Sunday. That Sunday, our pastor lifted a Bible high in the air and declared, "This is your voter guide. It instructs us to vote for those who are peace-loving, mercy-showing, justice-working, community-building, resource-sharing, creation-caring, enemy-reconciling, neighbor-attending, godly, wise leaders. Consult this as you prepare to cast your vote." The people of God are not owned by a political party.*

*Following the presentation of this chapter's contents at a university chapel service, students posed several questions to the author. These questions and the author's replies are available at http://www.facebook.com/CharitableDiscourse.

10

ALCOHOL

A few years ago, I was in Chicago with some friends. It was a hot, sticky day and we needed to get some exercise, so we went to a gym at the University of Chicago to play racquetball. The four of us played cutthroat racquetball until we were drenched, exhausted, and spent. Then one of my friends offered postgame beverages—a six-pack of Heineken on ice back in his room. We all trekked to his room, and I enjoyed my machine-cooled Coke while the three of them split the six-pack. My abstinence made the math easier. Dividing a six-pack by four is like figuring out who gets the last piece of pizza. We sat around and talked about our jobs, our families, our sports teams, and our faith. My three friends were an Episcopalian priest, a Lutheran pastor, and a Mennonite leader.

Are my friends sinners for guzzling the Heineken? Are they going to hell? Did they do damage to the cause of Christ that hot summer day?

If they were pastors of some conservative churches, they could potentially be fired by their church board. But in other denominations, their church board members would buy the beer.

Can we talk?

Let's start with an honest confession. You cannot make the case for total abstinence from alcohol by quoting verses from the Bible. Sure, there are scriptures about alcohol:

> Wine is a mocker, strong drink a brawler, and whoever is led astray by it is not wise *(Prov. 20:1).*

Who has woe? Who has sorrow?
Who has strife? Who has complaining?
Who has wounds without cause?
Who has redness of eyes?
Those who linger late over wine,
those who keep trying mixed wines.
Do not look at wine when it is red,
when it sparkles in the cup
and goes down smoothly.
At the last it bites like a serpent,
and stings like an adder.
Your eyes will see strange things,
and your mind utter perverse things.
You will be like one who lies down in the midst of the sea,
like one who lies on the top of a mast.
"They struck me," you will say, "but I was not hurt;
they beat me, but I did not feel it.
When shall I awake?
I will seek another drink" *(Prov. 23:29-35).*

Besides this, you know what time it is, how it is now the moment for you to wake from sleep. For salvation is nearer to us now than when we became believers; the night is far gone, the day is near. Let us then lay aside the works of darkness and put on the armor of light; let us live honorably as in the day, not in reveling and drunkenness, not in debauchery and licentiousness, not in quarrelling and jealousy. Instead, put on the Lord Jesus Christ, and make no provision for the flesh, to gratify its desires *(Rom. 13:11-14).*

Do not get drunk with wine, for that is debauchery; but be filled with the Spirit, as you sing psalms and hymns and spiritual songs among yourselves, singing and making melody to the Lord in your hearts, giving thanks to God the Father at all times and for everything in the name of our Lord Jesus Christ *(Eph. 5:18-20).*

But there are other texts that suggest a different understanding of alcohol. According to Num. 18:12, the priests get paid from the wine offerings. In Deut. 7:13 we are promised that if we obey the Lord, he will bless us and increase our wine production. In Deut. 12:17 and Neh. 13:5, wine is part of the tithe. In Ps. 4:7, the Lord is praised because he makes us happier than new wine. Psalm 104:14-25 thanks God for giving grass to cows and "wine to gladden the human heart" (v. 15). Paul tells young Timothy to be careful about drinking the water and to take a little wine for his stomach (1 Tim. 5:23). Jesus manufactured fine wine for a wedding in Cana (John 2). He was also called a glutton and a drunkard for eating and drinking with sinners (Matt. 11:19; Luke 7:34). Apparently he did not abstain. The Communion cup of the New Testament was not Welch's Grape Juice.

The biblical record is clear. Drunkenness is strongly prohibited, but total abstinence is neither commanded as law nor practiced as a rule.

So why the call to total abstinence?

I think you would agree with me that the use of alcohol in our day is different from the days of Scripture. Our proof power in the distillery is much higher than theirs. We can get people drunker, faster. Surveying the effect of alcohol simply on eighteen- to twenty-four-year-olds in the United States, we know the following:[1]

- 1,400 per year die in alcohol-related accidents.
- Over 500,000 are unintentionally injured under the influence of alcohol.
- Over 600,000 are assaulted by someone who has been drinking.
- More than 70,000 students are victims of sexual assault or date rape in which alcohol is involved.
- About 25 percent report negative academic consequences linked to alcohol use.
- 2.1 million students drove under the influence of alcohol last year.
- Alcohol dependence and abuse cost the United States an estimated $220 billion in 2005—more than the cost of cancer and obesity.
- One-third of all deaths from fire or drowning are attributed to alcohol.
- Booze is the blame of many divorces.
- Alcohol often triggers spousal abuse, child abuse, and raging tempers.
- Alcohol damages the liver, the kidneys, and the pancreas.
- Alcohol use robs US businesses of an estimated $90 million in lost production.
- In New York City, an estimated 1 in 5 tax dollars is spent dealing with the effects of substance abuse.

- Two-thirds of American teenagers will drink and somewhere between 8 and 12 percent of them will become problem drinkers or addicted to alcohol.
- 1 in 10 people have a genetic predisposition to alcohol addiction.

We know in a general way that alcohol has an adverse side effect in our society, but many among us know it in a more personal way.

- The police officer who, one more time, smells it and administers the roadside sobriety test.
- The medical doctor who examines the liver and sighs.
- The social worker who clicks the pocket camera and captures the bruises for a record of drunken abuse.
- The counselor who reaches for the Alcoholics Anonymous (AA) phone number.
- The high school teacher lecturing to dazed minds, and the college professor who knows she will never penetrate the alcohol-induced fog.
- The child who wonders whether this Christmas will be like the last one, with parents behaving badly.
- The wife who listens for the sounds that will reveal whether he is coming home drunk or sober.

As a pastor, I've done the funerals of three teenagers killed by drunk drivers. The scars on these families are still there. Marriages are in limbo, and pain lingers near the surface of these lives. I have wept with families whose wage earner spent it all at the bar and there was nothing left for groceries. From my friends in Russia, I've learned that vodka is cheaper than windshield washer fluid by decision of the government and that many people just put it in their windshield washer tank. My Russian friends also tell me that alcohol abuse is tanking their economy because it erodes the work ethic of the people.

Not long ago I received news that my friend Robin died at age forty-nine. He was the best children's soccer coach in the community, a friend to everybody, a greeter at the church door who knew every name, a neighborhood organizer, a kind and gracious man. They found him facedown in the dirt beside a river. He had drunk himself to death. He could conquer anything in life except a bottle.

Having seen all this, I chose to say no to alcohol on behalf of my fellow humans. Logic tells me that the world might be better off with less folk drinking and more folk abstaining. Even the alcohol companies are calling for moderation and not letting friends drive drunk. They even contribute to the programs that help the addicted, such as AA. The social standard is one of moderation, self-discipline, and personal discernment.

So why the call to abstinence?

As the people of God, we are guided by our story. Our formative narrative is found in the Old and New Testaments and is the most reliable picture of who we are to be. I find an interesting story in the correspondence of Paul with the Corinthians. His instructions cast light on the issue of alcohol.

The Corinthians had grown up in the social world of the gods—Zeus, Aphrodite, Dionysus. Ornate temples were erected for the worship of these gods. Cultic celebrations were commonplace. Animals were sacrificed to the gods, the meat cooked, and the meal served to gathered people. The more sacrificial meat they ate, the more "filled" with the gods they were. Eating the idol meat was a social event. These events were connected to craft guilds, marriages, and cultural banquets. But when the gospel of Jesus came to Corinth, the question of eating sacrificial meat was raised. The Jewish story suggested that animal sacrifices were connected in the Old Testament to the worship of the one true God. And the "Spirit-filling" of interest to Christianity was not the spirit of the gods but the Spirit of the resurrected Jesus. Some said, "It's OK to eat the meat." Others said, "This is wrong." So Paul wrote,

> Now concerning food sacrificed to idols: we know that "all of us possess knowledge." Knowledge puffs up, but love builds up. Anyone who claims to know something does not yet have the necessary knowledge; but anyone who loves God is known by him.
>
> Hence, as to the eating of food offered to idols, we know that "no idol in the world really exists," and that "there is no God but one." Indeed, even though there may be so-called gods in heaven or on earth—as in fact there are many gods and many lords—yet for us there is one God, the Father, from whom are all things and for whom we exist, and one Lord, Jesus Christ, through whom are all things and through whom we exist.
>
> It is not everyone, however, who has this knowledge. Since some have become so accustomed to idols until now, they still think of the food they eat as food offered to an idol; and their conscience, being weak, is defiled. "Food will not bring us close to God." We are no worse off if we do not eat, and no better off if we do. But take care that

this liberty of yours does not somehow become a stumbling block to the weak. For if others see you, who possess knowledge, eating in the temple of an idol, might they not, since their conscience is weak, be encouraged to the point of eating food sacrificed to idols? So by your knowledge those weak believers for whom Christ died are destroyed. But when you thus sin against members of your family, and wound their conscience when it is weak, you sin against Christ. Therefore, if food is a cause of their falling, I will never eat meat, so that I may not cause one of them to fall *(1 Cor. 8:1-13).*

Paul is suggesting there are two arguments in play. The argument from knowledge says we all know there is really only one God and that the idol gods do not really exist. So the sacrificed meat has no divine power in it and we are free to partake. Our possession of such knowledge allows us to handle this issue without violating our faith in God. In a similar vein, it might be argued that while knowing the potential for damage from drinking alcohol, we have sufficient knowledge to handle the practice. We will drink responsibly and not harm others.

The second position could be called the argument from love. While we may have liberty and freedom in the issue, we will not use our freedom in a way that might harm others. We do not wish to "sin against [the] members of [our] family, and wound their conscience" (v. 12). This is the main argument of Paul in the issue of eating meat sacrificed to idols. Knowledge has the tendency to puff up, while love has the tendency to build up. One harms the church and its weaker members; the other is sensitive to them and restrains freedom for the sake of love. One is used to rationalize personal behavior on the basis of personal rights; the other is rooted in a community ethic designed to protect the weak.

Given this understanding, the alcohol question might be posed like this: "Will I use my freedom to drink to do as I please? Or will I limit my personal liberty for the sake of others?"

The issue of rights is one that Paul, as a minister of the gospel of Jesus, is quite familiar with. He continues:

Am I not free? Am I not an apostle? Have I not seen Jesus our Lord? Are you not my work in the Lord? If I am not an apostle to others, at least I am to you; for you are the seal of my apostleship in the Lord.

This is my defense to those who would examine me. Do we not have the right to our food and drink? Do we not have the right to be accompanied by a believing wife, as do the other apostles and the

> brothers of the Lord and Cephas? Or is it only Barnabas and I who have no right to refrain from working for a living? Who at any time pays the expenses for doing military service? Who plants a vineyard and does not eat any of its fruit? Or who tends a flock and does not get any of its milk? Do I say this on human authority? Does not the law also say the same? For it is written in the law of Moses, "You shall not muzzle an ox while it is treading out the grain." Is it for oxen that God is concerned? Or does he not speak entirely for our sake? It was indeed written for our sake, for whoever plows should plow in hope and whoever threshes should thresh in hope of a share in the crop. If we have sown spiritual good among you, is it too much if we reap your material benefits? If others share this rightful claim on you, do not we still more? Nevertheless, we have not made use of this right, but we endure anything rather than put an obstacle in the way of the gospel of Christ. Do you not know that those who are employed in the temple service get their food from the temple, and those who serve at the altar share in what is sacrificed on the altar? In the same way, the Lord commanded that those who proclaim the gospel should get their living by the gospel *(9:1-14).*

Paul has established that he has rights. Apparently, these rights have been contested by the Corinthians, and Paul has defended his rights on the basis of common logic. He has equal rights to room, board, a traveling companion, and the expectation of salary. But he will not insist on those rights if they hinder the message of Christ. After stating this, he moves immediately back into the issue of sacrificial meat:

> But I have made no use of any of these rights, nor am I writing this so that they may be applied in my case. Indeed, I would rather die than that—no one will deprive me of my ground for boasting! If I proclaim the gospel, this gives me no ground for boasting, for an obligation is laid on me, and woe to me if I do not proclaim the gospel! For if I do this of my own will, I have a reward; but if not of my own will, I am entrusted with a commission. What then is my reward? Just this: that in my proclamation I may make the gospel free of charge, so as not to make full use of my rights in the gospel.
>
> For though I am free with respect to all, I have made myself a slave to all, so that I might win more of them. To the Jews I became as a Jew, in order to win Jews. To those under the law I became as one under the law (though I myself am not under the law) so that I might

> win those under the law. To those outside the law I became as one outside the law (though I am not free from God's law but am under Christ's law) so that I might win those outside the law. To the weak I became weak, so that I might win the weak. I have become all things to all people, that I might by all means save some. I do it all for the sake of the gospel, so that I may share in its blessings *(vv. 15-23).*

The same principle that leads Paul to organize his life for the sake of the unbelieving Jews, those under and outside the law, leads him to order his life for the sake of the weak, that he may win the weak. The weak are defined as those whose conscience is wounded when they see the brothers and sisters who claim "knowledge" eating the sacrificial meat. Paul appeals to the example of an athlete:

> Do you not know that in a race the runners all compete, but only one receives the prize? Run in such a way that you may win it. Athletes exercise self-control in all things; they do it to receive a perishable wreath, but we an imperishable one. So I do not run aimlessly, nor do I box as though beating the air; but I punish my body and enslave it, so that after proclaiming to others I myself should not be disqualified *(vv. 24-27).*

Paul is willing to live under a discipline that enables him to win the race he competes to win—the establishment of the people of God under the belief that Jesus is Lord. As Paul's argument continues into chapter 10, he draws on a chilling warning from the Older Testament narrative of a time when eating and drinking led to the practice of idolatry among the people:

> I do not want you to be unaware, brothers and sisters, that our ancestors were all under the cloud, and all passed through the sea, and all were baptized into Moses in the cloud and in the sea, and all ate the same spiritual food, and all drank the same spiritual drink. For they drank from the spiritual rock that followed them, and the rock was Christ. Nevertheless, God was not pleased with most of them, and they were struck down in the wilderness.
>
> Now these things occurred as examples for us, so that we might not desire evil as they did. Do not become idolaters as some of them did; as it is written, "The people sat down to eat and drink, and they rose up to play." We must not indulge in sexual immorality as some of them did, and twenty-three thousand fell in a single day. We must not put Christ to the test, as some of them did, and were destroyed

by serpents. And do not complain as some of them did, and were destroyed by the destroyer. These things happened to them to serve as an example, and they were written down to instruct us, on whom the ends of the ages have come. So if you think you are standing, watch out that you do not fall. No testing has overtaken you that is not common to everyone. God is faithful, and he will not let you be tested beyond your strength, but with the testing he will also provide the way out so that you may be able to endure it.

Therefore, my dear friends, flee from the worship of idols. I speak as to sensible people; judge for yourselves what I say. The cup of blessing that we bless, is it not a sharing in the blood of Christ? The bread that we break, is it not a sharing in the body of Christ? Because there is one bread, we who are many are one body, for we all partake of the one bread. Consider the people of Israel; are not those who eat the sacrifices partners in the altar? What do I imply then? That food sacrificed to idols is anything, or that an idol is anything? No, I imply that what pagans sacrifice, they sacrifice to demons and not to God. I do not want you to be partners with demons. You cannot drink the cup of the Lord and the cup of demons. You cannot partake of the table of the Lord and the table of demons. Or are we provoking the Lord to jealousy? Are we stronger than he?

"All things are lawful," but not all things are beneficial. "All things are lawful," but not all things build up. Do not seek your own advantage, but that of the other. Eat whatever is sold in the meat market without raising any question on the ground of conscience, for "the earth and its fullness are the Lord's." If an unbeliever invites you to a meal and you are disposed to go, eat whatever is set before you without raising any question on the ground of conscience. But if someone says to you, "This has been offered in sacrifice," then do not eat it, out of consideration for the one who informed you, and for the sake of conscience—I mean the other's conscience, not your own. For why should my liberty be subject to the judgment of someone else's conscience? If I partake with thankfulness, why should I be denounced because of that for which I give thanks?

So, whether you eat or drink, or whatever you do, do everything for the glory of God. Give no offense to Jews or to Greeks or to the church of God, just as I try to please everyone in everything I do, not seeking my own advantage, but that of many, so that they may be saved *(10:1-33).*

So what conclusion does Paul reach? He refuses to view the eating of the sacrificed meat as an act of evil, unless the one who does so is a participant in the worship of demons. Paul also says that it is wrong for one with a "weaker conscience" to impose it as authoritative on the one who eats the meat. The call is to act in the best interest of the other. This means that the one who recognizes the harm being done by eating sacrificial meat will not eat it, and the one offended by eating the sacrificial meat will not demand abstinence of those who eat with a clear conscience.

Translated to alcohol, those who abstain will not pass judgment on those brothers and sisters who drink while belonging to the family of God. And those who see the harm being done by alcohol may, in love for others, choose to abstain.

I do not drink. My lifetime drinking is confined to an Episcopalian Communion service in which wine was used. Personally, I hated the taste. Friends tell me it is acquired. I have no interest in acquiring a taste for spinach either. If I did like the taste, I believe I could drink responsibly. I think I would have enough personal discipline to know when to stop. But I chose not to drink as an expression of loving concern for my fellow humans. I belong to a radically subversive movement attempting to destabilize social drinking by not participating. I want my choice to empower others to say no. I do not seek to pass judgment on those who drink responsibly, nor make them feel guilty by my action. When asked why I don't drink, I simply explain that having seen the damage that alcohol has done to people I've known and loved, I am acting in solidarity with their best interests.

This position rises from the core of Wesleyan-Holiness theology, which calls us to love God with our entire being (to the point of ordering our lives for the sake and pleasure of this God) and to love our neighbor in redemptive ways.

Your choice about alcohol will probably fall into one of three categories:

1. If you experience no relationship with God, you will most likely do as you please. You will drink if you want to. Or you will not drink because you hate the taste, have health issues, or find sense in the logic of the dangers of alcohol on our society.

2. You, as a believer, will drink responsibly (as is your right, unless your conscience condemns you or another is harmed by your action). You have "knowledge" and your "conscience" permits you to do so.
3. You will not drink based on an ethic of love for your neighbor.

To those who drink, be careful. I ask you to reconsider your position for the sake of your neighbor. To those who abstain, be careful. Your attitude toward your fellow Christians should not be arrogant, haughty, or superior. And be ready to explain without judgment why you chose to say no.

And my three friends with the Heinekens? One lost his congregation the following year and went into an alcohol recovery program. One had a teenage daughter arrested for drunken driving. The other one is doing just fine.*

*Following the presentation of this chapter's contents at a university chapel service, students posed several questions to the author. These questions and the author's replies are available at http://www.facebook.com/CharitableDiscourse.

11

HUMAN SEXUALITY[1]

One story of human sexuality goes like this:

"Sex is good—very good. We are created to enjoy sexual experiences. People who frown on sexual activity need to get a life. Narrow-minded Christians are just shoving their prudish beliefs down our throats. Who are they to tell us what we can and can't do with our own bodies? Sexual abstinence is antiquated. Virginity is outdated and overrated. To expect anyone to wait until they're married is unreasonable and cruel. As long as you protect yourself from unwanted pregnancy and disease, it's your body. Do as you please. Now, you shouldn't hurt anybody or do anything against their will. But what two consenting people do in private is nobody else's business. The most important thing is that you click with the other person. Sex is a way of your telling them that the relationship is going somewhere—unless you make it clear that this is just recreational sex with no strings attached, just being friends with benefits. It's important to be honest about where you're coming from. It's true that people get hurt sometimes. One wants to stay together—the other wants to leave. But that's the risk you take. Always be as kind as you can when you're breaking it off. But remember—this isn't marriage—it's just sex, and if it stops being good for you, you're free to leave. Sex is a basic human need. No one has the right to deny you your rights. It's your body and you ought to be able to do with your body what you think is right for you."

Ever heard that story? It's embedded in almost every song, movie, novel, TV show, blog, YouTube video, billboard, magazine, and talk show you encounter. It's everywhere. And it has penetrated American culture to the degree that few challenge the basic assumptions anymore. I wish to challenge the core of this story and offer a better one in its place.

Assumption 1: Sex Is Good

I agree. I agree wholeheartedly without reservation. Some Christian studies have gone as far as statistical analysis on the matter of whether Christians have better sex than the rest of the world. These studies are cute, and maybe make a point, but I'm not sure they are useful to the Christian story. I'm not sure the game is won by the side that proves it has the best sex. Do we really want to compete at pure hedonism? And if we win, what have we proved?

Sex is good, but it is not the essence of life. Sex is wonderful, but it is not the most wonderful thing about being human. Sex is not the goal of relationships. Sex is not even a basic human need. It is a desire, a craving, a want. It is not a human need. Food, air, water—those are human needs. I have yet to do the funeral of anyone who died from a lack of sex or to see it as the cause of expiration on a death certificate.

Intimacy is a need. Do you remember the movie they showed us when we were kids in school, *Cipher in the Snow*? It's the story of a child who rode the bus every day, and then one day, just died. They could find no cause of death. But when they began to unveil the pattern of this child's life, they found that no one ever touched, loved, spoke to, cared for, or called the child's name. It's a sad story about a child who died for lack of intimacy.

Our world has confused sexual intercourse with intimacy. The entertaining world of stories (books, TV, movies) has led us to believe that intimacy leads to sexual activity. In every show, you see it coming. You know when the characters are introduced that they will soon be in bed with each other. The mystery is gone. It's as predictable as the people we live with. When we automatically connect human intimacy with sexual behavior, we have bought into a script that is hard to extract ourselves from.

If intimacy and sexual behavior are essentially one and the same, I suppose one of our favorite virgins, Jesus, must have lived half a life. I would also suggest that another of our favorite virgins, Mother Teresa, missed the essence of life as a lonely, loveless, half-person. The idea that human intimacy is fulfilled only in sexual intercourse is a leap of disastrous proportions. Jesus, Mother Teresa, and a lot of my single adult friends are the most alive people I know. The need is not sexual intercourse; it is intimacy—to be known, loved, touched, understood, and cared for.

Sex is good. Yes. Yes. Yes. God created the first nudist colony. Trinity is not ashamed of naked human bodies. In the Garden of Eden, God saw it all and said, "This is good." God's no prude. Christians shouldn't walk around blushing when the topic of sex comes up. This is the gift of our Creator. But I think when we begin to connect the need for human intimacy with sexual drive and assume that these two are automatically and inextricably linked, we are in the wrong story.

Assumption 2: "Sex Is a Private Matter Between Two People"

For the Christian the distinction between a private life and a public life does not exist. Our thoughts, feelings, emotions, fantasies, and actions are a help or hindrance to the people we live among. To say that sex is a private matter between two people is a misunderstanding of the covenant life of the Christian. What we do is everybody's business! The health of our relationships depends largely on the way we live our most personal lives in service to our fellow human beings.

Most Christians have not yet comprehended this. We don't understand it. Early in our walk with God, we assume there is an ethical difference between deeds done in public and in private, and we place primary emphasis on public deeds while minimizing the impact of private deeds. But what a Christian does in private is everybody's business. Now I am not making the case for total vulnerability to the paparazzi, removal of curtains and boundaries, or the tell-all rags that adorn the grocery store checkouts. Privacy is to be respected as an act of human decency. What I'm suggesting is that our private lives have public consequences.

Sin says, "My life is mine, and I can live it the way I want, and it's nobody's business what I do with my own private body in my own private time." If you believe this, the discipline of sexual abstinence until marriage will make absolutely no sense to you. You will consider it an imposition from the outside, infringing on your personal freedom. Sin rises in us all to defend our self-sovereignty. Sin logically opposes the Christian story, because to accept it and to live in it requires that we die to self-sovereignty and yield to an authority rooted in something very different from living for the self. The law of God exposes this sinfulness in us by our reaction to it.

But law is not where our Christian story begins. Act 1 is not the giving of law on the holy mountain. God didn't jet in, lay down law, and leave: "Here are the rules. No adultery, no cheating on your wife, no rape, no lusting after women, no sexual immorality, and no sex before marriage. I'm gone, but I'll be back to judge you on these rules." This is not the way law came to us. Law is part of a larger story of a Creator's loving care for creatures. The story goes like this: "Once upon a time Creator created creation. Creator loved his creatures stubbornly. These creatures violated the relationship they had with their Creator. They seized what they wanted instead of respecting the relationship. Creator refused to dump them, overpower them, or manipulate them, and so the Creator became a creature—flesh and blood—and lived lovingly alongside them until they crucified him one day. But this did not exhaust his love for them. Creator's love continued and formed a community called church. And in this church Creator taught people to live and love as Creator himself had lived and loved among the people. And in this community there was no lusting, no using, no breaking promises, no violating—only faithful bonding in family and godlike intimacy."

This our story—and we're sticking to it. The law is a snapshot of the love of God. It is a movie of what life in Christian community is like. Beneath every law is a hidden promise full of life. And everything we do, in public and private, is an expression of the life of this God. In private, we are practicing the person who lives publicly.

Assumption 3: "Sex Is Just Sex, Nothing More"

Sexual intercourse is more than a physical act. According to Scripture, it creates a bond between two people. Two become one. Two bodies become one body. In God's definition, a man leaves father and mother and he is joined to his wife, and the two become one flesh (Gen. 2:24). It's a miracle. The mystery of it is akin to the reality of one God named Trinity who is comprised of Father, Son, and Holy Spirit. Three are one, yet the one is three. In sexual intercourse, something of the body and spirit of one person attaches to the body and spirit of another person. It is an encounter between two people in which each does to the other something that cannot be erased. You become an ongoing part of the person. You are defined by your relationship with that person. Each gives something that cannot be taken back. Sex leaves an indelible imprint on the soul of another person. And the stamp of that other person becomes a part of who you are. You are one flesh. Paul said it clearly in his letter to the Corinthians: "Do you not know that whoever is united to a prostitute becomes one body with her? For it is said, 'The two shall be one flesh'" (1 Cor. 6:16).

So what's wrong with premarital sex?

We are attaching ourselves to someone to whom we do not intend to stay bound.

Jerry worked with me at the Alamo Plaza Motel in Nashville. We were both working our way through college. He was a student at Vanderbilt; I was a religion major at Trevecca Nazarene University. He worked the afternoon/evening shift, 3:00 to 10:30 PM. I came on for the night shift, 10:30 PM to 7:00 AM. I would check in the late guests and do the evening transcript of the day's accounts. He would often let me know that if I needed him for anything, he would be back in room—pick a number. He had checked in a guest and had gotten an invitation to her motel room after his shift was over. His intention was to score. Many nights he would return to the office with a woman's panties, his trophy for an evening of conquest. He proudly hung the conquered apparel in his storage closet.

I remember the night he came into the office and slumped on the couch. I was working on the night transcript, and he began muttering to himself, meaning to be overheard by me. "I don't get it. Here you are a virgin, dating a great girl, never had sex and don't intend to until you're married. I've had more women than I can remember. You feel loved and valued. I'm miserable and lonely. I don't get it." It must have been divine inspiration that hit me in the middle of the night. "Jerry, I do get it. You are destroying your capacity to love. Every night, you practice bonding and breaking, bonding and breaking. Sexual intercourse binds two people in a covenant of marriage for life. It is a bonding act. When you bind yourself to a person that you hardly know and walk out of the room never intending to see the person again, you damage your capacity to love. You are learning to love and leave, not love and stay. It doesn't surprise me that you feel lonely. You've been doing nothing but using your fellow humans and treating women like conquests in a game. My goal for sex is to love and stay, bind myself in marriage to one person and stay bound for the rest of my life. Call it boring. Call it conservative. I call it love as God intended it to be." I don't know if my motel sermon moved him or not. But I still believe what I said that night.

The world would say that Jerry was experienced, and he was. He was experienced at bonding and breaking, using and leaving, holding and walking away. He did it so many times it became the core of who he was. He was using people for what he wanted, and his little closet was a memorial to the humans who had submitted to his conquest. It's no wonder that he sat slumped in a seat in the middle of the morning saying, "I don't have any friends. I don't even know how to love anymore." He had violated his own soul so often that he had lost his capacity to love.

Assumption 4: "Nobody Is Getting Hurt"

"It's private. It's nobody else's business. Nobody else is getting hurt." I beg to differ. When you choose to practice bonding and breaking, using and leaving, holding and walking away, you are damaging your own capacity to love another human being the way God has loved you. You're harming something deep in your being in exchange for a moment of hedonistic pleasure.

No one's getting hurt? I beg to differ. As a pastor I've logged time listening to human stories. A trail of tears has left watermarks on my life. I've listened to stories of unplanned pregnancies and abortions, disease, date rape, acquaintance rape. I've listened to confessions of the use of pornography, which turns women and children into objects of sexual pleasure. I've listened to testimonials of sexual addictions. I've seen middle-aged wives dumped by Daddy for a younger model. I've seen breakup, regret, depression, low self-esteem, adultery, ruined reputations. I've watched homes torn apart, children of divorce, and friends you can't invite to the wedding. I've counseled the fallout from the moment the fiancé says, "Did you? And who?" I've lived long enough for my teenager to look at me and ask, "Did you?"

The sexual story of our world has created more pain than almost any other evil.

But of all the stories I've heard, the one I've never heard is, "We regret that we waited to have sex until our wedding night." I've never heard that. But I have seen a premarital couple come in for a talk, then a few days later one of them sheepishly calls and says, "I don't know what to do about this. There are these other people, and I know he/she is going to ask me. It's kind of embarrassing. The people I had sex with are our friends. How do I tell him/her? Do we invite them to the wedding? I don't think I can walk down the aisle." And at the end of the conversation they usually say, "I'd give anything to have that night back. I'd give *anything* to have that night back." I've seen that hurt and that pain.

We're not hurting anybody? Get real! We are hurting each other with our sexual behavior. And the price tag we're paying is destroying people's lives. The world's sexual ethic is the story of selfish quest, use and abuse, and destruction. The story of God's people is a story of intimacy, covenant love, binding and staying bound, loving "till death do us part." That is the story of the people of God.

Which story are you in? Which story are you practicing? Which story has claimed you?

"I'm going to do what I want to do with my own body, and hopefully nobody gets hurt; but if they do, it's a risky world out there. I can love and leave if I need to."

Or

"I'm going to make a commitment to one person in this world that I will make to no other person in this world. I will demonstrate the kind of faithfulness to that person that God has demonstrated to his people down through history when he said, 'Don't go after other gods. I love you like no one else can love you, and I want you to be secure in this relationship with me.'"

Which of these stories do you want to define your life?

My favorite definition of evangelism is "telling someone into a better story." God is at work getting us into a story called the Love of Trinity. Father, Son, and Spirit are like a beautiful dance. Movement between the partners is the essence of the dance. Another image is music composition. The beauty of the music is not in the individual notes, but in their relation to one another. The beauty of this love within Trinity is meant to shape how we love. Rather than using a body selfishly, we reverence and respect it for the sake of God. When created beauty becomes the idol we fix our eyes on, it becomes the tomb that enslaves us, because we are no longer free to receive it as a gift of the Creator. It is amazing how lust-love drops its eyes immediately from the face to the sexual organs. We no longer see the face filled with the soulish expressions of feelings, moods, joys, sorrows, thoughts, and delight. We just look at the body parts incapable of any unique message or expression. "There are no more *Mona Lisas* in art, and at this point it seems doubtful that there will be any in the future. Feminine beauty is entirely reduced to a means of seduction (sex appeal), to the grave detriment of women themselves, who end up being seen only in relationship to men as objects and not as persons."[2] Our quest is not the love of beauty, but the beauty of the love we have seen in the Trinity.

Some of us know the story and are characters in it. Some of us have never heard it—yet. We are being embraced as the objects of God's love, and we don't even know it. We're out there writing our own script and doing it our own way. And God knows the end of that story is Jerry, slumped on a couch, having used up all the people he can use up, with a closet full of conquests. We sit there atop our pile of experiences, lonely. No one really knows us, no one really loves us, and no one really cares about us—except God. And when we get to the end of having used everybody else, God is the only one left who will not try to use, manipulate, or overpower us—but simply wants to love us. And when we experience this love, our sexual ethic changes, because we're living in a different story.

The relationship God has given me with my wife, Denise, is a priceless gift. One night, we sat together watching the closing scenes of *Titanic* in which the main character, Rose, is letting her savior-lover go, and he's sinking into the cold, deadly sea. They had made promises to one another. And then, decades later, as an older woman, she returns to the spot, goes to the edge of the ship, and drops the priceless Heart of the Ocean blue diamond into the waters. As the diamond of their romance sinks, life erupts in a kind of resurrection scene of love. The ship is restored, all the dead are raised, and beauty returns to the deep.

I was reminded of the love my wife and I share. We were brought together in a moment in time. We would give a great priceless pearl to the ocean for the privilege of walking through life in loving intimacy. Sex within marriage is wonderful, a tremendous gift. And the marriage we have today began when we were sophomores in college. While we were dating, we learned to love and respect the boundaries of clothes. We learned to be intimate in ways not sexual. We learned self-discipline. We learned that our sexual behavior would mean something to our families then, to the family we now have, and one day to our grandchildren and their families. We learned that our love would serve congregations, families, and premarital couples. I wouldn't take anything for the grace and guidance of God in that time in our lives, because who we are today was being formed inside us as we were bound together by God.*

*Following the presentation of this chapter's contents at a university chapel service, students posed several questions to the author. These questions and the author's replies are available at http://www.facebook.com/CharitableDiscourse.

12

HOMOSEXUALITY

Once upon a time homosexuality was little more than a joke, a rare mention, or a suspicion. Now it is a day-to-day reality. The issue is before us, out of the closet. We have friends and relatives, coworkers and church leaders, who, in one way or another, are dealing with homosexuality. It is in the newspaper, on TV, and in our schools. The issue divides people and churches. It is tearing apart friendships, congregations, and homes.

Our initial reaction to homosexuality may be one of anger, denial, or repulsion. At one time, homosexuality was dismissed as immoral by a dominant majority. It was simply wrong. And some went even further with name calling. Words like "fag," "queer," "dyke," "queen," and "fairy" were attached to our fellow humans with the same recklessness that "glutton," "drunkard," and "friend of sinners" were attached to Jesus. Homosexuals found themselves as the butt of jokes or clichés. "It's Adam and Eve, not Adam and Steve." This kind of response is neither helpful nor Christian.

As a pastor, I have sat face-to-face with those who struggle with sexual orientation. Some were broken and empty; others were angry and militant. Allow me to offer some of their questions and statements along with pastoral responses informed by Wesleyan theology.

1. What about the person who wrestles with an orientation he or she did not choose?

Our biblical and theological understanding of sin suggests it is both personal and corporate. We personally choose to sin and are accountable to God for the willful choices we make. Sexual orientation is not a willful choice. Sexual behavior, acting on our orientation, is. There is a clear distinction between orientation and behavior. One is sinful; the other is not. Being heterosexual is an orientation, not a choice. It is neither moral nor immoral. Behaving heterosexually or homosexually in relationships with the opposite/same sex *is* a moral issue.

We also recognize sin as corporate. The fallen world in which we live affects us in multiple ways. As Americans we become greedy because we are formed in a materialistic consumer society. We didn't wake up one morning and decide to be greedy. We were born into a greedy world, and this sticky sin stuck to us.

Whatever the cause of homosexual orientation, it reflects a fallen world. Like greed in the world, it is something we are called to respond to out of the redeeming grace of God. The person who is homosexually oriented does not need a church that condemns his or her orientation but a church that calls for a response in keeping with the character of God. The church should not be a place of ridicule and condemnation, but a place of love, grace, and redemption. We must walk the fine line between welcoming the homosexual and accepting/condoning homosexual behavior.

2. Why is homosexual behavior wrong?

God has created us with the capacity for faithful, loving relationships. Marriage is the epitome of such relationships and is likened to the Trinity by the apostle Paul. The love of Father-Son-Spirit is a self-emptying, giving, bonding, other-preferring love. As humans, we are carefully crafted and intentionally designed to bond in covenant relationship. Our bodies have a functional form, and this includes our sexual organs. God created us to fit together as male and female. This "fittedness" is biological but also psychological, emotional, and spiritual. Men and women are created to desire each other and are physically equipped to act on that desire. We preach and teach that sexual union is God's gift for marriage, and through this physical act, a lifelong covenant of devotion is celebrated. Sexual union is not haphazard and casual but is an expression of life bonding.

Given the reality that the overwhelming occurrence of homosexual behavior is neither monogamous nor intended to establish a God-honoring lifetime relationship, we believe that such behavior is destructive in the same way that premarital heterosexual union harms the persons involved. They are practicing the art of loving and leaving, bonding and breaking, using and walking away, without intent to remain faithful. God does not love like this, neither should we.

In most homosexual behavior, sexual union is not viewed as a covenant-making, life-bonding experience. It lacks the commitment that goes along with intimate connection. People are using each other's body as objects, relating to each other as things, as instruments of gratification. Homosexual behavior destroys the human capacity to relate to another and remain whole. It is relational suicide. It destroys the sacredness of human relationships. When we use each other sexually without the depth of marriage commitment, we are being less than human.

The logic that condones homosexual behavior is innately selfish. This logic claims that homosexual desires are natural and that a person has the right to act on his or her natural desires. "I want what I want regardless of others, regardless of what it does to society, regardless of what it does to me or to my family."

We all have selfish desires; but this does not mean that we give ourselves to those desires. To the contrary, Christians are ultimately called to discipline desires, to lay down our lives for others, and to bear the fruit of the Spirit, which is self-control. The pit of selfish sexual pursuit is easy to fall into and hard to crawl out of. Its patterns dig tracks in the soul. Homosexual behavior damages a person, a relationship, a family, and a world. Choosing to practice a lifestyle regardless of its consequences is ultimately selfish.

3. "I'm a practicing homosexual Christian."

A person who makes such a claim is making two statements: (1) I am a practicing homosexual, and (2) I am a follower of Jesus Christ. Which one supersedes the other? Which one is most basic to one's identity? If a person is first and foremost "Christian," then his or her sexuality bows in obedience to Jesus Christ. If a person is first and foremost "homosexual," then God takes second place to sexual orientation. If a person's sexual identity supersedes his or her identity in Christ, that identity is idolatrous. Anything above God is an idol.

4. What is the call of God for Christians who are homosexually oriented?

Remember the distinction between homosexual orientation and homosexual behavior. Homosexual *orientation* is the inclination to desire sexual intimacy with a person of the same sex. Homosexual *behavior* is achieving sexual gratification with someone of the same sex. The first is a *desire*; the second, an *action*. No one chooses to be a homosexual, but one does choose whether or not to engage in homosexual behavior. The call to the Christian homosexual is the same as the call to a single Christian heterosexual—to live a life of disciplined sexual abstinence.

5. Can a person who is homosexually oriented be reoriented to heterosexuality?

Sometimes. There are homosexuals who testify to healing grace that transformed their sexual orientation. The reality, however, is that this is not always the case. My pastoral experience suggests that about 30 percent who are homosexually oriented have been reoriented to heterosexuality. And most of these occurred in cases where teens or young adults were able to receive skilled counseling early in their journeys and were supported by strong Christian friends. Dealing with one's sexual orientation calls for professional counseling. Those who are not reoriented are called to live a life of abstinence enabled by the work of the Holy Spirit in their lives.

6. How do we show God's grace to homosexuals without condoning their lifestyle?

There are two wrong responses. The first is to naively believe that homosexuality is a simple matter to be fixed by one serious trip to the altar. Such naïveté on our part underestimates the pull of the homosexual orientation. When this attitude is taken, the church ends up offering simplistic remedies that compound the frustration of those who struggle with homosexuality. The second wrong response is to believe that homosexual orientation is irreversible and thereby offer no help. This response surrenders to pro-homosexual rationales that are called biblical but are far from it. The result is to join our sister denominations who are beginning to sanction the homosexual lifestyle as acceptable, though not desirable, or even accepting the homosexual lifestyle as completely natural and acceptable.

Neither of these is an adequate response. Instead, our response to homosexuals must mirror that of Jesus. He went out of his way to find and associate with the rejected, the outcast. He was a friend of sinners (including pagan Gentiles like you and me). He ate with them, offered them acceptance, and told them the good news of the gospel. He invited them to share in his life. Jesus offered good news to captives, recovery and freedom to the oppressed, and proclaimed to them the blessing of the Lord. The church must continue in that work.

Our greatest failure as the church is to imagine that a homosexually oriented person can live a celibate life without the benefit of Christian community. We are created for human intimacy. We need human touch, conversation, inclusion, belonging, and care. Counseling a person in the office or at the altar is not the end of his or her struggle. It is a battle waged in the trenches of that person's daily life. The homosexual has real needs. He or she is asking, "Who do I talk to? Eat with? Play with? Share holidays with? Celebrate birthdays with? Who hugs me? Listens to me when I am sad? Calls me? Thinks to include me? Where do I live? Who do I live with?"

If the church wants to get serious about helping the homosexually oriented person live a celibate Christian life, we must think in terms of gracious, rich hospitality. Christian singles will purchase large houses that become havens of belonging for men and women to live in God-honoring community. Families will permanently open their homes to a new member of the family. Churches will develop support groups and provide mature mentors. The celibate single homosexual will be invited to full participation in the life and ministry of the church. We cannot expect a person to go off and cope with this and then come back when he or she has it settled. One of our best means of grace is the fellowship of the church. We must offer it to all.

If the homosexual community offers a better welcome than the people of God, a struggling person will seek help from that community. If we, as the church, immediately condemn our homosexual brothers and sisters without taking the time to get to know them, we will turn them away from the church and from God. Homosexuals need the church, and they matter to us, because they matter to God.

God's grace belongs to the homosexually oriented, and the church should be the bearers of this gift. The church is called to lovingly and caringly build bridges toward people, as Jesus did. We are called to compassion toward the homosexual, and compassion involves telling the truth about homosexuality, its roots, and its consequences. We must not shy away from either of these tasks. The people of God may be the only place left where homosexuals can be loved and hear the truth of God.

7. What does the Bible have to say about the practice of homosexuality?

Writers like Robbin Scoggins and John Boswell have written books based on their exegesis of Scripture and concluded that the Bible does not oppose the practice of homosexuality. They believe these texts deal with males using young boys as prostitutes.

Congregations calling themselves the Metropolitan Community Church have adopted this exegetical position and have become a haven for practicing homosexuals. Other mainline congregations have decided that the practice of homosexuality is not sinful and have called for monogamous relationships among gay and lesbian couples. Some have sanctioned marriages between these couples.

In all honesty, we should be slow to condemn these congregations. They are our brothers and sisters in Christ and have gone through deep pain to reach the place of acceptance. Their loving acceptance of those who are homosexually oriented has saved many from the unprincipled gay community where anything goes. And I would submit that given the choice between the practice of random sex with multiple sexual partners and a monogamous lifetime relationship with one partner, their call to monogamy is much to be preferred over the alternative.

But let's look at the texts in question:

> You shall not lie with a male as with a woman; it is an abomination *(Lev. 18:22).*

> If a man lies with a male as with a woman, both of them have committed an abomination; they shall be put to death; their blood is upon them *(Lev. 20:13).*

The laws of Leviticus are rooted in the holiness of God and connected to Israel's destiny as the people of God in the land that has been given to them. The verses in view prohibit the sins of sexual promiscuity—adultery, prostitution, homosexuality, and bestiality. These sexual unions are in violation of the "one flesh union" described in Genesis. These texts concern life in the land as the blessed people of God. It is interesting that this section follows the section on blood. Life fluids are the primary interest here, especially as they pertain to procreation of the people of God. Nothing is to challenge the bonding that forms family and raises children who are heirs to the promises of God. The sexual sins mentioned destabilize the family as God intended it. And to label these acts as abominations is to connect them to the idolatrous practices of surrounding tribes. The people of God are to be different.

It is true that many of the Levitical laws are no longer practiced by the followers of Jesus and that their fulfillment has occurred in different forms under the teachings of Jesus. We do not sacrifice animals to obtain forgiveness, and we do eat pork. So we look to the New Testament to see how the issue is addressed:

> Do you not know that wrongdoers will not inherit the kingdom of God? Do not be deceived! Fornicators, idolaters, adulterers, male prostitutes, sodomites, thieves, the greedy, drunkards, revilers, robbers—none of these will inherit the kingdom of God. And this is what some of you used to be. But you were washed, you were sanctified, you were justified in the name of the Lord Jesus Christ and in the Spirit of our God *(1 Cor. 6:9-11).*

Paul is addressing a heresy present in the Corinthian church. Some believed their exalted knowledge and their superior spiritual state disabled the moral rules by which the community was formed. They had enlightenment excusing them from the law. They were free to do as they pleased. And they did. The divisive issues ranged from eating meat sacrificed to idols[1] to disruptive babbling in worship to questionable sexual ethics.

In this text, Paul uses two different words: *malakoi*, which refers to the passive partner in homosexual activity, often a young boy; and *arsenokoitai*, which is translated by the NRSV as sodomites. This word is usually translated homosexuals, and for good reason. *Arsen* (men) + *koitus* (bed/sexual intercourse) = the sexual intercourse between men. It is clear in this text that Paul is dealing with more than the use of young boys as temple prostitutes. He is speaking about male homosexuality.

And the continuation of the practice is not imaginable for Paul. The people have been washed, sanctified, and justified. This is who they used to be and are no longer. They are now called to glorify God in their bodies:

> For the wrath of God is revealed from heaven against all ungodliness and wickedness of those who by their wickedness suppress the truth. For what can be known about God is plain to them, because God has shown it to them. Ever since the creation of the world his eternal power

> and divine nature, invisible though they are, have been understood and seen through the things he has made. So they are without excuse; for though they knew God, they did not honor him as God or give thanks to him, but they became futile in their thinking, and their senseless minds were darkened. Claiming to be wise, they became fools; and they exchanged the glory of the immortal God for images resembling a mortal human being or birds or four-footed animals or reptiles.
>
> Therefore God gave them up in the lusts of their hearts to impurity, to the degrading of their bodies among themselves, because they exchanged the truth about God for a lie and worshiped and served the creature rather than the Creator, who is blessed forever! Amen.
>
> For this reason God gave them up to degrading passions. Their women exchanged natural intercourse for unnatural, and in the same way also the men, giving up natural intercourse with women, were consumed with passion for one another. Men committed shameless acts with men and received in their own persons the due penalty for their error.
>
> And since they did not see fit to acknowledge God, God gave them up to a debased mind and to things that should not be done. They were filled with every kind of wickedness, evil, covetousness, malice. Full of envy, murder, strife, deceit, craftiness, they are gossips, slanderers, God-haters, insolent, haughty, boastful, inventors of evil, rebellious toward parents, foolish, faithless, heartless, ruthless. They know God's decree, that those who practice such things deserve to die—yet they not only do them but even applaud others who practice them.
>
> Therefore you have no excuse, whoever you are, when you judge others; for in passing judgment on another you condemn yourself, because you, the judge, are doing the very same things. You say, "We know that God's judgment on those who do such things is in accordance with truth" *(Rom. 1:18—2:2).*

This text is not primarily about homosexuality but about the righteousness of God. The good news is that God is reaching to fallen humans with the intent of saving them from death. Paul makes the point that we are not merely ignorant of God's saving intent but that we know exactly what we are doing when we sin. We are refusing to acknowledge God as God. As a result we have become darkened in our thinking. We've turned from the worship of God to the worship of created things. We have twisted God's intent for his creation by our perversions. God's wrath is that he permits us to have our way. He gives us over to the consequences of our sin. Homosexuality is one illustration of this.

In homosexuality, we exchange God's created intent (one flesh male/female bonding in a covenant of marriage) for our own same-sex preference, which is contrary to nature as God made it. But before we begin grading sins, we must remember that sins of equal seriousness are also in this list of illustrations—envy, gossip, slander, deceit, rebellion against parents. It's all on the list. Shall we begin expunging the church roll of all gossips?

And the more serious warning is levied in Rom. 2:1-2. In passing judgment on others, we condemn ourselves. In some ways Paul sets a trap for his Jewish readers. After whipping them into a moral frenzy about all the immoral things the Gentiles do, he puts their judgmental attitude in the same category of "sins under the wrath of God." He is saying that we are all guilty and in need of mercy.

Other biblical texts mention homosexuality in lists of sins to be avoided. Various interpretations of the word are "sexual immorality," "sodomy," and "homosexual offenders."

Given these texts, one can conclude that a practicing homosexual is welcomed in the church to the same degree that a gossip or envious person is welcomed. The community of Jesus welcomes sinners. If they are not welcomed, then none of us belong. But this does not mean that the call to holiness is set aside. To welcome and to condone are two different things. I would even say that to excuse sinful behavior is an unloving act toward a person for whom Christ died.

In the same way that we call the single heterosexual to the practice of virginity and abstinence, we call the homosexually oriented person among us to the same. Celibacy is not a fate worse than death. Sexual gratification is neither a basic human need nor a right to be protected. It is the gift of God for the covenant of marriage.

For those who are practicing homosexuals, the call of the church is transformation. Paul's language to the Corinthians is clear—this behavior is who they used to be and no longer are. To make an exegetical case that the Scriptures do not prohibit the practice of homosexuality is to read the Bible through rose-tinted glasses of assumed self-authority.

A Closing Word

The church can take two postures toward the person wrestling with the practice of homosexuality. Both are found in the parable of the prodigal son. One is the posture of the father, waiting at the gate in hope that the son will come home from a life of destruction. The other is that of the elder brother, grousing about how rotten and undeserving the abominable brother is.

To the practicing homosexual I would say, you have no excuse for your sin. I have no excuse for my sin. You need the same mercy I have found in the cross of Jesus. You did not choose your orientation, and I place no blame on you for it. The church is trying to understand the complexity of your relational perceptions and emotional needs. I do not think your challenge is easy. I do not believe we can "fix" you. That is a presumption that is cruel. You need enormous grace, true friends, biblical truth, and God's help to enable you to live a whole and rich life. I pledge to love you as I believe God loves you.*

Biblical Study Resources: Homosexuality

The following books and articles are recommendations for those wishing to educate themselves about biblical texts dealing with homosexuality.

Dawn, Marva. "Homosexuality." Chap. 9 in *Sexual Character*. Grand Rapids: William B. Eerdmans Publishing Co., 1993.

Furnish, Victor. "Homosexuality." Chap. 3 in *The Moral Teaching of Paul*. Nashville: Abingdon Press, 1979.

Gagnon, Robert. *The Bible and Homosexual Practice: Texts and Hermeneutics*. Nashville: Abingdon, 2002.

Hawthorne, Gerald F., Ralph P. Martin, and Daniel G. Reid, eds. "Homosexuality" in *Dictionary of Paul and His Letters*. Downers Grove, IL: InterVarsity Press, 1993.

Hayes, Richard B. "Awaiting the Redemption of Our Bodies: Drawing on Scripture and Tradition in the Church Debate on Homosexuality." *Sojourners Magazine* 20 (July 1991), 17-21.

_____. "Homosexuality." Chap. 16 in *The Moral Vision of the New Testament*. San Francisco: HarperCollins Publishers, 1996.

Schmidt, Thomas. *Straight and Narrow? Compassion and Clarity in the Homosexual Debate*. Downers Grove, IL: InterVarsity Press, 1995.

Stafford, Tim. *Sexual Chaos: Charting a Course Through Turbulent Times*. Downers Grove, IL: InterVarsity Press, 1993.

---

*Following the presentation of this chapter's contents at a university chapel service, students posed several questions to the author. These questions and the author's replies are available at http://www.facebook.com/CharitableDiscourse.

13

HOMOSEXUALITY *letters from the* SILENT PEWS

Each time I publicly address the issue of homosexuality, I receive letters from those who struggle with their sexual orientation. These are not people who are trying to cram an agenda down the throat of the church, nor are they evil. They are dealing with an issue that many of us have just begun to comprehend. And their pain is evident.

I share these letters to offer voices other than my own in the conversation. These were college students attending a Christian university in Illinois. Their names and identities are changed and details of their biography altered, but the letters appear as they were written.

January 23

Dear Pastor,

I have wanted for a while to write and thank you for your sermon on homosexuality. It was a wonderful, accurate, courageous, biblical sermon. I'll tell you why I think so.

I am a female religion major here who struggles with homosexuality. Just so you know, we've never met, so don't go mentally searching through the female religion majors you know to see if you can guess which one I am. I wouldn't want to pin this on any of them. I only tell you what major I am so that you will know that there are those of us struggling with this in every field, even religion. I hope to be in full-time ministry someday, but homosexuality is still a problem for me.

I have never engaged in any homosexual activity directly, though I am a current pornography addict, which is related to my homosexual issues. I am working to overcome the pornography addiction.

Though debates exist about whether or not homosexuality is genetic, I do not believe in my case that it is. Incidentally, I appreciated your honesty in your sermon in saying that we really don't know whether or not it is genetic. That is the scientific truth. I also appreciated your saying that it doesn't exactly matter whether or not it is genetic: God has still forbidden it, and God can still give us the strength to deal with celibacy. I truly and deeply believe that myself.

Back to my own case . . . I don't at all think it's genetic. I come from a background of abuse on both sides of the family for generations, awful physical, verbal, and sexual abuse perpetrated by men of the family, often in the name of Christ using perverted Scripture. I learned early in life not to trust men. They had deeply hurt nearly everyone I knew, and that's no exaggeration. Though not through abuse, my father, one of the only men I ever trusted, deeply hurt me, but not until later in my life, in college. Perhaps most importantly, I was sexually abused when I was six years old and again when I was eleven by a different individual. Keep in mind that in addition to the distrust created by personal abuse, I lived in a climate of extreme distrust of every single man. Those especially suspect were those we should have been able to trust, family and pastors, which were usually one and the same. Add to that the complication . . . that I was extremely distant from my mother. Though I am not sure of the reason for that distance, I believe that it was due to my anger over her allowing me to be abused the first time.

All of this makes a dangerous combination. As you said, homosexuality typically, if not always, is a sexualizing of emotional needs. My Christian therapist, whom I began seeing at age fifteen and ceased seeing last November, always said that every homosexual she had ever encountered had been abused. These people have their natural sexual desires blocked due to emotional, usually sexual trauma, so their natural sexual desires turn to the only option left, the same sex. This is usually accompanied by deep issues with their parents, usually a lack of connection with their same-sex parent, which creates a profound emotional need. This emotional need gets all wrapped up with the sexual needs that are already confused by the trauma.

So you see, I had all of these things in my life, and I do believe that that's what caused the homosexual struggles in my life. Understanding the origins of the desires is helpful, but it doesn't change them. I can know all I want to about it, but the fact is I still feel the same way; I still react the same way.

Can I tell you what being a Christian who struggles with homosexuality is like? Two things come to mind: self-loathing and loneliness. We don't want to feel this way. I would guess every homosexual would say that, but I know every Christian who struggles with homosexuality would. We hate our reactions. Often we hate ourselves. I don't think most heterosexuals know or understand that. We would rather die than ever feel something about a friend, and I assure you if we're caught off guard with such an involuntary reaction, we turn away, close our eyes, shake our heads, and turn our thoughts elsewhere so fast that we scarcely know it happened because we want that even less than our friends ever could. We are as horrified by such a thing as they ever could be, and we don't let our thoughts dwell there. There are exceptions, I'm sure. There was a girl here at school that I could easily have been in love with, and I guess I thought a lot about that, but I was deeply disturbed even by that. The vast majority of the time we don't feel that way or allow ourselves to think that way.

The other idea that comes to mind is loneliness. Maybe this is the biggest feeling I've experienced. It is loneliness clear down to my bones. It really began to hit at college, especially as I began to care about that girl I mentioned. As I began to crave a relationship, any relationship, more and more, I realized not only that I would never have a relationship with that girl but that I would never have a relationship with any woman. At that time, that was the only relationship I could conceive of. I knew, in faith, that God could heal me. However, I didn't know if he would, and if he would, when. Though spiritually I could believe things might be different, emotionally and mentally I could not imagine how things could ever change. As I saw it, I was facing the prospect of being alone forever.

A single person always has the possibility that God will bring someone into [his or her life]. For someone struggling with homosexuality who can't imagine being anything else, it doesn't feel like there's any hope that [he or she] will ever find someone. That's loneliness. Though it is celibacy by choice, in some ways it's not a choice, because that's not what we want. We want relationships, and they're out there to be had, relationships we can imagine, relationships we want, but we can't have them. That's hard.

I do not know what I would tell anyone who did not already believe in the love and power and comfort of God. I would be very bitter with God if I didn't already know him. Why does God forbid something that to us seems very natural? Why would God deny us such profound desires of our hearts? If anyone thinks homosexuality is primarily physical, they're wrong. It's so much more than that. But I know that God only forbids us things that are bad for us, and I can trust that. Nonetheless, emotionally, it is excruciating. I feel like I have a pretty strong faith, but it has been so difficult. It requires constant dependence upon God.

The other reason it is so lonely is that it is so isolating. We're trying to deal with all of these feelings, all of these struggles, and we have to do it alone because our greatest fear is rejection. The last thing we need in this struggle is rejection. The church is the worst, and that's so scary. We need them, but we're scared of them. They, of all people, will condemn us. Even if people are engaged in an active homosexual lifestyle, they still need help, not condemnation, and those of us wavering really need to be bolstered, not pushed over the edge. People struggling with homosexuality are already profoundly hurting, and they need the healing touch of Christ, the love, grace, acceptance, and forgiveness the Church can offer—not more guilt and pain. Trust me, we're feeling plenty of guilt as it is.

My biggest fear is not the people who would outright reject me. I know who those are in my life, and I just don't tell them. No, my biggest fear is a more subtle form of rejection, those in my life who would still love me but who would struggle. Oh, I understand their struggle, I do, and I'm not angry, but it still hurts. I worry if I tell someone, especially a female, that she will go back through everything I've ever said and done wondering if I meant something by it. I worry that she will wonder every time I look at her, every time I touch her, every time I say something to her, that she will be afraid I'm feeling attracted to her. I worry that she won't touch me anymore, and I so crave touch, just hugs.

Even if our friends are wonderful enough to truly and fully accept us, and I have some like that, it's still lonely. My friends don't understand. I have never talked to someone who really understands my great pain and hollowness, my frustration, my failures. My friends don't want to hear about it on a regular basis because they can't handle it. Even if they can handle it, they don't want to hear about it day in and day out, but that's how I struggle with it, every day. Depending on God is vital, but hard. Sometimes it just doesn't seem to be enough.

What you said in your sermon was very balanced. We need to hear that it's wrong. So many churches are waffling or telling us it's OK. I wish they knew how difficult that is for us. I want more than anything for it to be OK. I barely hold on to that truth much of the time. To have a church tell me that it might be OK is so difficult. It makes me want to move there and attend there and pretend for the rest of my life that I can be a Christian and a homosexual without any problems. But I can't.

I appreciated, on the other hand, the way you encouraged the church to love us, to be friends with us. You are very right that that's exactly what we need. Thank you for being a voice of both truth and love. It was very courageous of you, in more than one way, for you to say what you did. The church, sadly enough, could easily have judged you for the love and acceptance you insisted they offer. The world, I'm sure, is outraged at your stand for truth that is not politically correct. But I thank you for that. I personally was wavering in the stand I had taken. I needed to hear again that it was wrong. I do not typically attend your church, but I came to hear your sermon like a woman in the desert looking for water. Thank you for giving me what I needed, for giving lots of people what they needed.

Your sermon prompted me to do some intensive Greek scriptural exegesis. I did it for one of my projects for school this year. When I finish writing it, I will send it to you. I do not mean to presume that you cannot do such research yourself. Perhaps you already have. However, perhaps you have not had a chance or reason to do such research. I have not had the training you've had, but I do have five semesters in Greek, and I feel that my exegesis is sound. I hope to do more research soon, just for my own self. I needed to do the research myself so that I could settle for myself once and for all that homosexuality really is scripturally wrong. I did settle that. I will send you what I learned when I finish it. It may not help you, but then again, it may.

Thank you again,
"Ella"

February 18

Dear Pastor,

For the past couple of weeks I have been thinking about coming in to talk with you about some issues in my life, but I was hesitant. After hearing your sermon yesterday, I decided to write to you about my best friend.

To make a long story short, after he graduated college and moved out on his own, he gave in to his loneliness and desires and soon found himself totally immersed in the gay lifestyle. The statistic about a large percent of gays having over one thousand partners sounds ridiculously overblown, yet I know it's true. My friend had around sixty partners in about four months.

Last year is when it started. After the first couple of months, he made up his mind to tell me. I was the first person he told. He was my best man at my wedding, yet he was scared to death to tell me. He knew there was a good possibility, in spite of our friendship, that I would turn my back on him.

Well, to his great delight, I said it wouldn't affect our friendship, and it hasn't.

Here's the problem, though . . . he's in a major crisis over his spiritual beliefs. And there's little I can tell him he doesn't already know. He's no intellectual chimp. He was a religion major . . . graduated at the top of his class . . . was praised by the faculty . . . and went on to seminary where he got involved in the gay community. This is a highly intelligent guy, knows the Bible thoroughly, and yet is faced with a personal "flaw" as he sees it, which the church condemns.

I can't tell him to pray, seek God's will, find counseling, join a support group . . . you see, he's *done* all that. For the past year or so he's been "white-knuckling" it as he calls it, fighting his desires with all his will, and constantly praying. Over that year he's had some of the closest encounters with God in his life . . . yet now I'm afraid the fight has left him exhausted, on the verge of surrender. He no longer feels the driving sexual needs but now seeks a warm, intimate relationship with a person.

He's on the verge of surrendering completely to the gay lifestyle, including switching churches to one that accepts homosexuals, although discarding Christianity also seems to be on his mind.

I'm the one he turns to when he has problems, and I feel I may be the only one who may be able to steer him back to Christ.

I don't know how to help him. He feels God may have made him that way, and not only will he not let him live the gay lifestyle, but he [also] won't help him overcome it. It's been a long, hard fight for him, and I don't know what I can do.

"Fred"

April 23

Dear Pastor,

After experiencing both sides of the fence in the struggle with homosexuality, I can honestly tell you that more long-term satisfaction is found in Christ than in sexual intimacy with the same sex. Ironically, many homosexuals do find their yearnings for identity and acceptance pacified through the gay life.

It felt wonderful when the weight of self-hate was lifted after I allowed myself to grasp the homosexual life. I found an overwhelming abundance of acceptance for who I was. It didn't matter that I had a homosexual orientation. It didn't matter that I was raised in a parsonage and held some rather conservative views. It didn't even matter that I was a Republican. No matter what I revealed about myself, these homosexuals accepted me. The fulfillment I received through these friendships filled a void in my life that I thought would always remain empty. But the void wasn't filled for long. By the grace of God, I once again found myself longing for more. I wasn't satisfied in serving the god of homosexuality.

God has called me out of the homosexual lifestyle, but the inclination still remains. I don't know how long until the desires pass, or if they even will, but I do know that God has a plan for my life and will see me through. I also know that if it weren't for the prayers of family and friends, I would still be searching for fulfillment in the gay community.

When I first came to you two years ago, you revealed to me the unconditional love of Christ. I still see that in you today. I truly believe that Christ's love imparted through his Spirit and through his people can radically change lives. Thank you again for revealing Christ's love to me.

"Steve"

May 4

Dear Pastor,

The reason I am writing to you is because I am gay and nobody knows about it. I mean not my friends or family. I have sought counseling with a pastor friend and through a Christian counseling service. Each has helped but the problem, and it is a problem, never seems to go away.

One of the reasons a person might be homosexual could be the lack of a male role model. I believe this describes me. You see my father was never around. He was an alcoholic, and he cared more about staying drunk than his kids. I sought out the attention of men to replace and to hurt my father. Only it did *not* replace or hurt him because he never, and still doesn't, know about me.

Now to the point of the letter. I'm not sure what to do. I have asked Christ into my life, but it seems I disappoint him every time I go to places I shouldn't or do things that aren't good. I don't know how to escape. I have been dealing with this problem since I was about twelve years old. It's hard to tackle.

I know for a fact that the lifestyle is wrong! That is not how Christ wants me to live. I just don't know what to do anymore. I'm tired of leading a double life. I have worked in the church at home for quite a while. I have been youth president, taught Sunday school, and served on the church board, all the while living a sinful life. I'm tired. I want to serve God, but I don't know how to get rid of this skeleton.

I will not give you my name or box number. I can't let anyone find out about me. I'm a student here and am having a hard time living here. I mean, I have some friends, but the guys in my dorm don't talk to me at all. I take that back; two guys on my floor do say hi to me, but that's about it. I have no real male friends, and it's lonely. Do you think they can sense something different about me? If there [was] some way you could get a reply to me, it would be great, but I can't risk being found out. It's easier to write a letter to you than to sit with you and tell you all this. I know Christ loves me no matter what, but I can never live a Christian life while living with this in my heart.

I'm sorry about just writing this letter. Just pray for me, please. Thank you for listening to me.

"Matthew"

June 20

Dear Pastor,

I struggle with homosexuality and pornography addiction. Many factors in my childhood went into both of these struggles, including a broken relationship with both of my parents, pornography exposure, and sexual abuse.

My parents love me very much, but they are both very broken people coming out of very broken homes. Femininity has been degraded and devalued in my family for generations. Both my father and my mother bought into the idea that men were superior and taught it to me. I thought for many years that gender role issues were not a problem for me as they are for others who struggle with homosexuality because my gender issues were not external. My mother influenced me enough in that area that I have always looked like a girl. My gender issues were more internal. Everything that my father was—stoic, academically intelligent, quiet, logical, in control, and analytical—was right, superior, and better. Everything that my mother was—creative, emotional, spontaneous, and talkative—was wrong, not just different, but wrong. I was raised to be like my father.

My mother's life left huge holes in her, and most of my life she used me to try to fill them. As a result, my mother was not safe for me. She could not be my mother as long as I had to be hers, at least emotionally. I withdrew from her, which made her cling all the more tightly to me, which caused me to withdraw further and further. This left me with a desperate need for women, for a mother. My mother, however, did not like for me to have friendships with other women, and I learned that it was wrong for me to need women. I tried to stuff that need, which only made it grow and grow.

At some point in my childhood, I was exposed to pornography that we had around the house. When I was ten, I was again exposed to pornography that an older male cousin of mine had. From the time that I was exposed to it, pornography became a fascination and a temptation for me.

When I was ten, the cousin who owned the pornography began molesting me. Soon after, I learned that many men in my family were sexual abusers. The message that I heard was that no men were safe. It wasn't just my cousin who was dangerous. All men would violate me. My fear of and disdain for men became generalized to all men.

I first remember being physically attracted to a woman when I was about ten years old. That attraction to women continued to grow throughout high school, though I tried to date men. I was physically ill trying to date men, and I stopped trying at age seventeen. My attraction to women at this point was pretty generic—women on TV, women who walked by, [and so on]—but it was growing. I became a Christian at age eight and was raised in the church, so I knew homosexuality was wrong, but that didn't change how I felt.

When I came to college, I met a girl I'll call Grace. If my attraction to her had been physical at first, I think I would have caught it and nipped it in the bud, but that was not the case. I was emotionally enmeshed with Grace long before I acknowledged my physical attraction to her. After

 Nyack College Library

some time, though, I was forced to realize that I longed for a romantic relationship with Grace and not just a friendship. Thankfully, Grace was always interested in men. Because of that, I never told her about my attraction to her. Though it was painful to me that she was not interested, I was also very grateful for that. There was a time when I would have pursued a romantic relationship with her if she had been interested, even though I knew it was wrong.

As I faced the fact that I could not have a romantic relationship with Grace, I had to face the fact that I could never have that kind of relationship with any woman. Deep loneliness began to set in. It was such a hopeless loneliness. I longed for intimacy that I could never have. God had forbidden the only intimate relationship I could imagine—one with a woman—the relationship I thought I needed. Homosexuality felt natural and right to me, even though I knew it was not, and I did not understand why it was forbidden. I was angry with God for the pain I was in, even though I knew he had my good in mind when he forbade homosexuality.

As I got older, pornography continued to be a temptation. I was becoming bored with the sexual fantasies my own mind could produce. When I was twenty, I gave in to the temptation to look at pornography. It provided the sexual highs I was seeking and gave me a way to indulge my homosexual desires.

I continued looking at pornography off and on throughout college. I could go months without it in the beginning but would always return, more and more often as time went on, for intense days and weeks of looking at pornography for hours at a time. Meanwhile, Grace graduated and moved to another country, and I stopped corresponding with her.

My senior year of college, nearly two years after I began looking at pornography, I told two of my professors about my struggles with homosexuality and pornography addiction. They encouraged me to seek counseling and helped me find a good Christian woman to see.

My counselor has helped me learn to forgive those who have hurt me, including my parents and my abuser. She has helped me to understand the issues behind my struggles with homosexuality. She has taught me to identify the lies that I have believed about myself and to see the truth instead. She has shown me how much self-hatred I have harbored, where that comes from, and how I have expressed that against myself. The one single thing I have learned that has changed my struggle with homosexuality the most is that it is OK to need women. My counselor has taught me healthy, godly ways of needing women and of expressing those needs. God has given me two safe women that I can practice on in those professors, now good friends of mine, whom I first confessed to. I am also learning how God himself can meet my needs for a mother. As I am having more and more of my needs for women met in healthy, godly ways, my physical attraction to women and my need for inappropriate emotional enmeshment are diminishing.

In March of 2005 it will be two years since I have looked at pornography. At Christmas I saw Grace for the first time in three and a half years. Though it was a painful and emotionally complicated experience, I was pleasantly surprised to discover that I was no longer attracted to her. It was a very concrete sign to me of just how much healing God has brought about in my life. I still have some work to do with my counselor, but we will soon be done and are beginning to look ahead to how God may use my story to help others. God has done amazing things, and I know that there is more ahead. I am excited to see what it will be.

"In need of Grace"

In Closing

These are our sons and daughters. Their struggle and pain deserve more than pulpit grenades thrown their way and jokes made at their expense. They want to walk with God and are tortured by inner struggles over sexual orientation. They have asked us not to throw in the towel on the gay lifestyle, and they have confessed that they are lonely and in need of listening ears, good friends, and human touch. The body of Christ can provide these in a context that will sustain a life of celibacy. If we fail to, they will walk away toward those who are ready to introduce them to a deadly way of living.

14

SCIENCE *and* RELIGION

The octane on this issue has evolved (pun intended) during my lifetime. Toss the raw meat of a few choice words—"evolution," "origin of the species," "four-billion-year-old planet," "global warming"—in the middle of a group of Christians, and you'll have enough spontaneous combustion to heat the church.

May I share an honest confession? I almost didn't include this chapter because I am president of a Christian university. At Trevecca Nazarene University, we are willing to ask the hard questions and converse with a maturing generation. But I know that many people have already discovered all the answers they are willing to hear on issues of creation and science. They prefer not to be confused with new scientific facts. Their minds are made up. And sadly, a conversation will not be possible. And their decision about a college for their sons and daughters may be the way they affirm their convictions. But when our faith causes us to check our brains at the door, we have fallen far from the God who gave us the capacity for reason.

My dilemma as a college president is simple. Will I engage a young generation in an open-minded biblical conversation that welcomes scientific discovery, reasoned philosophy, and careful logic? Or will I ignore all of these in favor of an interpretation of creation that is barely one hundred years old and rooted in the fear of science?

Recently, two university professors wrote an opinion in *USA Today*. They are both Christians. Their article attempted to express their view that evolution is not fundamentally in conflict with orthodox Christian faith. They wrote,

> The "conflict" between science and religion in America today is not only unfortunate, but unnecessary. We are scientists. . . . And we are religious believers. . . . Like most scientists who believe in God, we find no contradiction between the scientific understanding of the world, and the belief that God created that world. And that includes Charles Darwin's theory of evolution. Many of our fellow Americans, however, don't quite see it this way, and this is where the real conflict seems to rest. Almost everyone in the scientific community, including its many religious believers, now accepts that life has evolved over the past 4 billion years. . . . So you would think that everyone would accept it. Alas, a 2008 Gallup Poll showed that 44% of Americans reject evolution, believing instead that "God created human beings pretty much in their present form at one time within the last 10,000 years." The "science" undergirding this "young earth creationism" comes from a narrow, literalistic and relatively recent interpretation of Genesis, the first book in the Bible. . . . Evolution continues to disturb, threatening the faith of many in a deeply religious America, especially those who read the Bible as a scientific text. But it does not have to be this way.[1]

Can we have a civil discourse about this? Is one's scientific viewpoint a litmus test for his or her orthodoxy? If one believes that God created the heavens and the earth, is he or she to be scorned by fellow Christians because his or her theory of "how" differs? Is one's theory of creation essential to salvation? Should this issue be dividing the church?

The issues are complex and you need a program guide to understand all the players. And sorting out pro and con on evolution is just the beginning. There are young-earth creationists who posit a world created instantaneously six to ten thousand years ago. There are old-earth creationists who believe the earth was created billions of years ago and has evolved slowly. There are intelligent-design folks who place God in the gaps where science cannot explain what happened. They use God to connect the dots between creation, science, and Creator, thus proving God's role in the origin of all things. There are random-chaos theorists who think it just happened over a long time with no guiding hand in the mix. There are random-design folks who believe creation happens randomly, but under the loving direction of a designer. There are neo-Darwinists who declare the whole thing too complex to suggest a designer behind the wheel. And there are biblical literalists who go no further than "God said it. I believe it. That settles it." And there are theistic evolutionists who believe God guided the creation by means of evolution. Lots of players are in the game with very different opinions.

One of the best presentations I've heard on this issue was a lecture by Dr. Tom Noble.[2] In his review of the historical relationship between science and religion, he suggested that the popular idea of continuous conflict is a myth. Modern science was founded in Christian Europe and rooted in the biblical understanding that God created the world ex nihilo, "out of nothing." Other than the brief conflict with Galileo and Copernicus, the orthodox church has stood in close agreement with modern science through the centuries. Even Darwin's work was accepted by the majority of mainstream evangelical scholars, including B. B. Warfield, James Orr, and Henry Drummond. It was only the later versions of Darwin, in particular the work of T. H. Huxley, that were opposed. Huxley intentionally interpreted Darwin's theory as a refutation of faith in God as Creator. His anti-Christian writings used Darwin's theory to promote skepticism. It was not Darwin but Herbert Spencer who turned evolution into an ideology of "survival of the fittest." Others, like Hitler's followers, used Darwinism to make the case for a master race. These anti-Christian interpretations of Darwin were based on atheistic philosophical assumptions and rooted in naturalism, which denied any miraculous intervention of God in science and history. But the original work of Darwin, while it raised questions about the interpretation of the Bible, was viewed as compatible with Christian belief by most conservative theologians.

It is a very late development that pits Darwin against Christian faith. The Calvinist-rooted fundamentalists reacted to Huxley's view that evolution was anti-Christian. The famous Scopes Monkey Trial (1925) is the event that pitted the two sides against one another and began the popular myth that these two have always been enemies.

Noble summarizes Denis Alexander, the leading Cambridge scientist and a Christian, who posits five positions that have defined Christians.[3]

1. Genesis 1—3 is a myth containing eternal truth that God created the world and that humans are sinful.
2. Genesis 1—3 is a mythological version of a historical reality in which humanity turned away from God.
3. Homo sapiens evolved as suggested by Darwin, and at a specific point in human history, God chose Neolithic Adam and Eve to know him, revealed himself to them, and established covenant

with them. They became the first humans aware of God and were made capable of living in relationship with God. They sinned and their sin affected all humanity.

4. Old-earth creationism suggests that some evolution has occurred, but that God created life and the major species, especially Adam and Eve.
5. Young-earth creation suggests that the earth was created ten thousand years ago in six days and that Adam and Eve were created on the sixth day out of the dust.

These five positions, with some variations, offer the wide array of belief that currently exists among Christians today. Supporters can be found for every position. Is it possible that any of these positions are acceptable within orthodox faith? Yes. But not all are acceptable within the confines of modern science. The fifth alternative requires a total denial not only of biology and cosmology but also of physics, chemistry, and the entire family of scientific inquiry. While this position may and should be afforded welcome among Christian theories, it must be stated that it is a denial of science as we know it.

One of the best current conversations is being carried on by the BioLogos Foundation. Francis Collins founded this group to promote the search for truth in both the natural and spiritual realms, seeking harmony between these different perspectives. Collins led the Human Genome Project and now leads the National Institutes of Health. He is also someone who takes his Christianity seriously and believes there is no incompatibility between his faith and his science. It is the hope of this foundation to change the discussion about evolution at Christian colleges. The foundation is organizing a series of faculty workshops, starting with one at Gordon College, a multidenominational Christian college in Massachusetts, at which biology and religion professors will talk about evolution and how it can be taught at Christian colleges.

The premises of most BioLogos writers are rooted in theistic evolution. The basic beliefs of theistic evolution are as follows:

1. The universe came into being out of nothingness, approximately 14 billion years ago.
2. Despite massive improbabilities, the properties of the universe appear to have been precisely tuned for life.
3. While the precise mechanism of the origin of life on earth remains unknown, once life arose, the process of evolution and natural se-

lection permitted the development of biological diversity and complexity over very long periods of time.

4. Once evolution got underway, no special supernatural intervention was required.
5. Humans are part of this process, sharing a common ancestor with the great apes.
6. But humans are also unique in ways that defy evolutionary explanation and point to our spiritual nature. This includes the existence of the Moral Law (the knowledge of right and wrong) and the search for God that characterizes all human cultures throughout history.[4]

In addition, BioLogos leaders have written several books about the teaching of evolution within Christian colleges and have an agreement with InterVarsity Press to publish the first in the series, and possibly additional titles. I would recommend the following books from BioLogos, plus a few others, for those willing to seriously investigate the issue:

Berry, R. J., and Tom Noble, eds. *Darwin, Creation and the Fall: Theological Challenges.* Downers Grove, IL: InterVarsity Press, 2009.

Collins, Francis. *The Language of God.* New York: Free Press, 2006.

Falk, Darrel. *Coming to Peace with Science: Bridging the Worlds Between Faith and Biology.* Downers Grove, IL: InterVarsity Press, 2004.

Giberson, Karl. *Saving Darwin: How to Be a Christian and Believe in Evolution.* New York: HarperOne, 2008.

_____. *Worlds Apart: The Unholy War Between Religion and Science.* Kansas City: Beacon Hill Press of Kansas City, 1993.

The church will be discussing these issues in the near future, if not already. The bulk of our Christian scholars/scientists are in a camp different from the bulk of our laity. And the battleground is most likely to be the minds of our youth. If there is a widening gap between Christian universities and local church pews, how will the church deal with the potential divide?

Collins suggests,

> It is time to call a truce in the escalating war between science and spirit. The war was never really necessary. Like so many earthly wars, this one has been initiated and intensified by extremists on both sides, sounding alarms that predict imminent ruin unless the other side is vanquished. Science is not threatened by God; it is enhanced. God is

> most certainly not threatened by science; He made it all possible. So let us together seek to reclaim the solid ground of an intellectually satisfying synthesis of all great truths. That ancient motherland of reason and worship was never in danger of crumbling. It never will be. It beckons all sincere seekers of truth to come and take up residence there. Answer that call. Abandon the battlements. Our hopes, joys, and the future of our world depend on it.[5]

I am not a scientist and do not seek to write as a scientist. I have no desire to defend any of the specific positions mentioned above, including evolution. I do not know how old the earth is. I cannot explain instantaneous creation out of nothing, nor can I walk you through the intricacies of evolutionary development. But I am a biblical scholar and a Wesleyan theologian and will write toward a position that may allow holy conversation to occur between people who occupy pews and those who sit in university classrooms.

In Wesleyan theology, we interpret Scripture through three specific lenses: tradition, reason, and experience.

Tradition

We listen to the ancient church and what Christians have believed from the past. We give dead people a vote by paying attention to their understanding and theology. In the current science-religion debate, we should go back in history beyond the past one hundred years to hear the close symmetry between science and religion. Most science was done by scholars rooted in the church. And where the church was wrong about science (a flat earth, the earth rotating around the sun, etc.), the church corrected itself. This is our tradition. Augustine of Hippo, writing centuries before Darwin was a gleam in his parent's eyes, wrote concerning Genesis, "In matters that are so obscure and far beyond our vision, we find in Holy Scripture passages which can be interpreted in very different ways without prejudice to the faith we have received. In such cases, we should not rush in headlong and so firmly take our stand on one side that, if further progress in search for truth justly undermines this position, we too will fall with it."[6] The current suspicion of science is new to the church. The foremothers and forefathers of our faith traditions were much more open to scientific discovery than we are. We should listen to them. This is our tradition.

Reason

God has given us the capacity to think, communicate, articulate, postulate, and examine. The basic components of scientific work are the gift of God. Some would even say that these capacities are what it means to be made in the image of God. For us to close our mind to scientific reasoning without using our best critical thinking is to refuse to use our God-given capacity for understanding. We already know how to do this with Scripture. We know that Jesus does not intend for us to pluck out an eye or cut off an arm or tie a millstone around someone's neck and throw him or her in the sea. We interpret these texts through our use of reason. We allow what we know and understand to inform how we read the Bible. Science helps us understand that the three-tiered universe of the Psalms is not spatially correct. A psalm does not lose its meaning because the earth is not floating on the primeval sea but rather hanging in space by force fields that the Old Testament could not fathom. Let us use our reason to converse about the creation of our world, the age of it, our own creation, and the means by which our world works. In matters so mysterious, we could be wrong. Science itself has often been wrong.

Experience

John Wesley developed much of his doctrine of entire sanctification and Christian perfection by listening to the testimonies of the early Methodists. He believed that God could be understood through the collective experiences of people. When different people testify again and again to a certain experience of God, it suggests that the experience is true, reliable, and genuine. It is similar to the Proverbs of our Old Testament. These are the observations of those who have watched human behavior and the consequences of those behaviors. The Proverbs are probabilities based on observations of the wise and the foolish.

This, in essence, is how science works. It observes repeated experiences and draws conclusions. If the same thing happens over and over, it postulates a law or pattern. As people who give strong credence to experience, we should be the last to close our minds to the propositions put forward by scientific experiment.

As I have listened to the current debate, I have noted the presence of a fear of surrendering a literal interpretation of the Genesis account of creation. The reasoning goes, "If we give in here and say it is a poem or a story or a myth, what's to say the virgin birth or resurrection won't be next?

And if this part of the Bible is fiction, how do we know that other parts aren't as well? We must defend the Bible." It's as if the creation account of Gen. 1 is where conservative Christians have determined to make a Custer's last stand.

From here the fear spreads to the creation of humans. "If we descend from apes, how are we made in the image of God?" And next it moves to theologies of the planet that are self-centered. "God gave it to us to use and dominate. When it is used up, God will come and take us all away to heaven and we'll leave this messed up place behind." Then it moves toward a fixed pre-known universe and historical determinism (which are necessary in a Calvinist theology). And our eschatology (belief in last things) mirrors the popular Left Behind novels, rapture theologies, Antichrist namings, and end-time predictions. Strands of fundamentalism + Calvinism + folk theology + fear + TV preachers + best-selling novels are woven into a popular belief that is as different from Wesleyan theology as soap is from turnips.

All this is rooted in one narrow way of interpreting the Bible.

Recently I came across an excellent book by John H. Walton, professor of Old Testament at Wheaton College. His take on the creation narrative is carefully articulated in *The Lost World of Genesis One: Ancient Cosmology and the Origins Debate*. Walton expresses an understanding of Genesis that has captivated me for years.[7]

He suggests that Gen. 1 is the account of God coming to dwell in his creation with his creatures. While the pagan stories of creation seem to imply that creation exists for the gods and that humans are meant to placate the gods, our story is quite different. God moves in a way to cause creation to function for the sake of his creatures. The biblical account narrates the activity of God *on behalf of* his creatures rather than forcing the creatures to appease their Creator or suffer the consequences.

The major contribution of Walton is his insistence that Gen 1—2 is not primarily about the creation of the material universe but rather about God making the world function for his purposes for humankind. The text is in keeping with the dominant strain of theology throughout Scripture—God has come to dwell among us. Walton suggests that the people to whom Genesis was addressed already believed God to be Creator. They needed no coaxing to believe in God as Creator. What they needed was to understand creation as a move of God to dwell among them as his people. Could it be that Gen. 1 is not a story about the creation of the material world but about God making the world he created into his dwelling place?

The creative moves of Gen. 1 have to do with causing the world to function—delineating time, weather, seasons, growing food, and reproduction of plants/animals/humans. God is setting up shop in Eden to dwell among his creatures. Before Gen. 1, God hovers above the deep. After Gen. 1, God walks and talks with his creatures in the most intimate ways. The capstone of the story is the seventh day, Sabbath, when God rests from his labors. The crisis of a chaotic universe has been brought to resolution by the creative work of God, who causes the cosmos to function in an orderly, stable fashion. The chapter is written as a one-week narrative of God structuring the universe to function properly, rather than chaotically. The climax of the week is Sabbath as God rests in his cosmic temple and dwells among humans. The seven-day narrative plot is intended to establish the Sabbath rest of God among his creatures and creation.

In some ways, this story reminds us of the inauguration of Solomon's temple. There was a one-week buildup to the entry of God's presence into the newly built temple. It has been carefully constructed over seven years to function as the meeting place between God and humans. There is intense interest that God be present in the temple else it would not be a temple. The parallels between the narrative of Gen. 1 and the temple are significant. In essence, Eden becomes the temple of God in Gen. 1 as Solomon's temple becomes the temple of God, the place of God's presence in creation.

This understanding of Gen. 1 does not superimpose our language, culture, and science on the text and force it to serve our interests. Sadly, we have taken our scientific theories to it and have superimposed them, looking for proof of the correct theory. We wish to prove that God created the world, not some random forces of chaos. But the people to whom the text is written could not have imagined a world that God did not create. They did not need to be convinced that God created the world. It was already assumed. What they did not understand was how God had come to dwell among them as a people for his purposes in the world. The Genesis story of Abraham and his family will flesh out how the God of the universe intends to do that.

So while we believe God to be the Creator of all things, Gen. 1 is not limited to being the story of material creation. It is mainly the story of God's dwelling. When we force scientific creation theories on Gen. 1, we are asking the text to answer a question that is not being asked. Genesis 1 is not about the time periods (seven consecutive twenty-four-hour days or 4.5 billion years) over which the material universe came into existence but about a movement in time when God created a functioning world, ordered according to his purposes, and came to take his Sabbath rest in the cosmic temple of creation. This strain of thought is heard throughout the Bible:

> Thus says the LORD: Heaven is my throne and the earth is my footstool; what is the house that you would build for me, and what is my resting place? All these things my hand has made, and so all these things are mine, says the LORD. But this is the one to whom I will look, to the humble and contrite in spirit, who trembles at my word *(Isa. 66:1-2).*

"Viewing Genesis 1 as an account of functional origins of the cosmos as temple does not in any way suggest or imply that God was uninvolved in material origins—it only contends that Genesis 1 is not that story."[8] We have plenty of scripture that does declare God the Creator of all: Col. 1:16-17, Heb. 1:2, Ps. 100. If we allow a scientific debate to interpret Gen. 1, we have given modern science more interpretive weight than the human author of the text and the community to whom it was written. Biblical scholars across the centuries have seen Gen. 1 as a rich and complex text with many interpretations. Putting modern scientific ideas into this ancient story distorts the meaning of the text, which is clearly about God's faithful and caring relation to the world, not the science of how that world came to be.

Another concern is the development of a much-too-small doctrine of creation. The doctrine of creation must be more than a literal seven-day interpretation or a big bang at the beginning. God *continues* to create because creation is rooted in God's *future* purposes, not God's opening act of mystery. If Gen. 1 is to be read literally, I prefer to read it as the seven-day story of God interacting with his already-in-existence, chaotic, death-bound, disordered creation—which may have been materially existing for billions of years in some form—and bringing order out of chaos for the sake of dwelling with his people. In this reading, Adam and Eve are historical beings, whose names are part of a Hebrew genealogy, who experience God as their Creator, but even more so, who now understand their role within creation. They are privileged to function as obedient creatures of God, subduing and ruling creation as his partners. One does not have to explain *how* the material world came to be to understand how the text works to tell the community this story.

Or in other words, Gen. 1 takes no position on the age of the earth or the method by which it came into existence. Thus we need not pass a faith verdict on young-earth, old-earth, evolution, or any other theory of the origin of the material universe. We can enter the world of science with our eyes open wide, and when science offers substantial evidence of a process or pattern in the universe, we simply thank God that his ways are becoming clearer to us than before. Christians need have no fear of scientific discoveries of the origins of the universe. Our belief is not rooted in the *how*, because Scripture has not chosen to reveal the how. Our faith is rooted in the reality and experience of the God who came to dwell, who has a purpose to redeem and restore all of his creation, and who stubbornly continues to create that future until Rev. 21 is realized—a new Jerusalem come down, all things made new, death forever done, and God's dwelling with his people forever. Interestingly, the last chapters of the Revelation picture the temple made by God in which the Lamb is its light, and all creation celebrates.

Are there lines of defense for Christian faith, places where we should stand without yielding? Yes.

- God as Creator of heaven and earth, Maker of all things.
- God as the origin of life, the giver of life, and the one who raises the dead. All that is alive is alive in God, from God, to God, and through God.
- Creation as ongoing rather than finished. God is "making all things new" (Rev. 21:5). This is rooted in the doctrine of creation and incorporates our redemption as well as our future resurrection. The greatest creative move will be the resurrection of the dead, which lies in our future. We are no more intended to read the Revelation of Jesus to John as a timetable for the end times than we are intended to read Gen. 1 as the textbook of the scientific origins of the material universe. Both are rooted in the creative work of God to bring all things to completion in himself and redeem all his creation.
- The historical fall of the human creature. This reality is a necessary part of the divine/human story.

This leaves us with a robust understanding of God as Creator. God creates the material world. "How" is open to discussion. God invites us to engage in inquiry as to his ways in the world. God moves toward a future designed to make all things new. We can marvel that rain falls, sun shines, crops grow, and seasons turn—all in orderly fashion that enables us to thrive in the world. We can stop working every seven days and know that we are living out the story of a God who is in control, so we need not be. We can view the earth as a good gift, meant to be cared for, not trashed. We can be humbled by the entrustment of our Creator to reveal his ways to us, accomplish his work through us, and to imagine his future within us.

So how does the Christian enter the conversation with science? We are free to discover. But when science crosses the line of exploration and observation and begins to suggest that there is no meaning or function intended in creation, we have a problem. Science cannot fathom the mind and purpose of God in creation. Nor can science tell us why we are here. There is no evidentiary way for this to be proved. When theories of evolution go beyond how species evolved to the purpose behind this evolution, they have entered a realm that is not science. They have become either philosophers or theologians. Our faith interprets the findings of science as the activity of a loving God.

In the words of Benjamin Warfield,

> We must not, then, as Christians, assume an attitude of antagonism toward the truths of reason, or the truths of philosophy, or the truths of science, or the truths of history, or the truths of criticism. As children of the light, we must be careful to keep ourselves open to every ray of light. Let us, then, cultivate an attitude of courage as over against the investigations of the day. None should be more zealous in them than we. None should be more quick to discern truth in every field, more hospitable to receive it, more loyal to follow it, whithersoever it leads.[9]

What we learn from science need not shake our faith in God. Our line of defense is not a scientific model for Gen. 1, but a confidence in the Creator God who has a loving purpose for his creation and intends to dwell with his creatures and redeem us. The greatest act of creation is yet to come—God making all things new.*

---

*Following the presentation of this chapter's contents at a university chapel service, students posed several questions to the author. These questions and the author's replies are available at http://www.facebook.com/CharitableDiscourse.

15

the EMERGING CHURCH

A few years ago, we were enthralled in battles over contemporary worship music, seeker sensitivity, multicampus churches, video venues, and casual worship attire. I'm guessing many churches are still waging some of these wars. Most churches lag behind the fads and wait for the issues to arrive on their doorsteps by way of the next generation leaving for the more hip church down the street. How often we've watched a church change "because we are losing our youth to the First Church of What's Happening Now"—only to make the changes after they are all gone. The people "left behind" (the faithful remnant not the un-raptured) hate the new ways but are willing to change to save the now absent youth. So declining churches are filled with people who are now hip—and hate it.

A few years ago I wrote the book *The Worship Plot* to address the worship wars. In the introduction I wrote,

> Even as I write, a worship war is going on somewhere in a church. Some of these wars are simmering. Some are sizzling. Pulpit or no pulpit? Drums or organ? Guitars—maybe, if we don't plug them in. High liturgy, low liturgy, no liturgy? Preaching in formal or casual attire? Hymns or choruses? And if choruses, how many repetitions? If hymns, can anybody explain "terrestrial balls" and "sacred throngs"? Use of movie clips or ban Hollywood from the sanctuary? Plainspoken words or PowerPoint sermons that seem to scream, "Pay no attention to that person behind the pulpit!"

The division of the Body of Christ over worship style is a sad chapter in the story of a grand people. While our story is about the Spirit who makes us one, our worship wars make us winners and losers—mostly losers.[1]

From the preface,

My concerns are many. It concerns me when a pastor adds drums and drama, thinking he or she has gone contemporary. It concerns me when people argue over stylistic changes to worship without ever engaging significant theological questions. It concerns me when worship leaders import megachurch worship models without running it through the grid of their own history and theology. It concerns me that the future generation of worship leaders (now sitting in classes, chapels, and congregations) has no strategy for unifying a diverse people in worship. It concerns me that undue congregational energy is spent on in-house worship change to the detriment of outbound compassion, justice, and mercy. It concerns me when brothers and sisters retreat to the worship bunker of personal preference and begin to lob grenades at the opposing bunker. It concerns me that the one event meant to celebrate our unity—common worship—is the event that fractures and splinters us. So, you can see, I have my concerns.

But I also have high hopes. The worship that occurs in most sanctuaries is great worship—not because we are brilliant—but because the people come to do the work of worship. And this work did not begin with an order of worship. It began in the heart of God, who is the self-emptying love known as Trinity. True worship is the fellowship of the Father who sends the Son who gives the Spirit. And even as this shared life flows to us, it flows back as the Spirit empowers the sacrifice of the Son on our behalf, as a pleasing response to the Father. Trinitarian theology guides our understanding of worship. We are not creating something new but rather stepping into a stream that began in the very heart of God.

I have written at a lay level, because I believe worship belongs to the laity, the people of God. Worship is about their offering in Christ through the Spirit to the Father—not about a platform performance. It is my hope that this book will find its way to the battlefront where worship wars are currently being waged. I hope to lower the octane of the discussion and increase the meaning of the conversation. I offer this book as a gift to communities that care about worship. Too many churches have been wounded by friendly fire. Maybe I can spare you a few wounds.[2]

That was the battle brewing during the seeker sensitive/contemporary music movement. The newest battle is over the emerging church. Its roots are found in a generation that is disenchanted with the materialism, cultural accommodation, and use of power in the existing church. They are reacting against

- mass-produced services marketed by megachurches
- platform entertainment from the best band in town
- boxed, prepackaged PowerPoint sermons
- multiple services run by off-platform directors barking orders into headsets with timed precision
- the lack of community
- twenty-seven paid staff pastors with roles stretching from preacher to parking lot manager
- nonparticipating consumer audiences
- the preacher as answer man rather than spiritual guide
- the use of propositional points over biblical texts
- the modernist tendency toward systematic linear thought over narrative
- the contemporary distance from the creeds of the past
- the uncontested assumption of authority among religious leaders

The interesting thing is that they are bothered by many of the same things that have given an older generation heartburn. They have reached back into Christian history to restore the church, while also daring to address the postmodern context. When these young thinkers read their Bible, they are captivated by the radical nature of the kingdom of God. They find their home in the story of Jesus and the kingdom of God, sometimes to the neglect of the broader witness of Scripture in the Law, the Prophets, and the Epistles. They are in love with the simple Galilean and his call to enter the kingdom of God. And they know their current church does not reflect that kingdom, especially in America.

The emergents have researched their lineage to discover missional courage rooted in the church of the martyrs. They embrace the ancient rites and rituals. They find themselves in ancient creeds. They embrace the pre-Reformation practice of the church as the center for the arts. They worship in less expensive buildings and, sometimes, give more money to the poor. They do not wish to support local church budgets where 50 percent of the money is lodged in pastoral salaries but prefer instead to do the work of the church under sparse pastoral leadership. They would rather champion a local cause than support denominational programs. They embrace the kind of social justice evident in the ministry of Jesus without capitulation to a political party. They embrace a theology of creation that calls for care of the earth rather than the more popular but less biblical end-time trashing of the planet. They dress down. They have no goal to become a church of one thousand or to be located in the wealthy, growing sector of the city. Some of them are poor theologians and wander into heresy and bad theology. Some are recycling the old, thinking they have found the new. Others are the best and brightest minds of the church and long for close connection with their theological tradition even as they chart new ways of being the people of God in the world.

One of the significant issues to be recognized in writing about the emerging church is that it is broad and varied. You can find heresy, and you can find some of the best theology being done in contemporary society. You can find social justice, and you can find artsy fluff. You can find great biblical preaching, and you can find leaders with new gadgets on an ego trip. And the same can be said of the traditional church in any denomination. Sadly, what many opponents label as emerging is "anything they don't like." The following review of the emerging church is overgeneralized, which is the only way to speak of the movement, unless you identify a specific local church or group of church leaders.

Several books have been written on the emergents.[3] Eddie Gibbs and Ryan Bolger[4] identify three core practices of the emergents: (1) identifying with the life and ministry of Jesus, (2) transforming secular space by dismantling the barrier between sacred and secular, and (3) living as community. From these core practices emergents welcome the stranger, serve with generosity, participate as producers of worship and ministry, create as creative beings, lead as a body, and participate in spiritual activities. Common themes include

- emphasis on the life we are now living versus going to heaven when we die
- tearing down the secular-sacred divide
- a thorough rejection of consumerism
- participation over consumption
- inclusion over nationalism
- expression of faith through the creative arts

- evangelism as love over proselytism
- ancient liturgy
- authenticity over relevance
- leaders as facilitators rather than authorities
- highly democratic decision making
- quiet and reflective atmosphere over decibel-shattering volume
- dimmed lights over strobe lights
- volunteers over paid staff

D. A. Carson[5] offers the following estimation of the emergent movement:

Strengths

- Reading the times—it is aware of the postmodern era and seeks to communicate to its context.
- A push for authenticity in relationships and community.
- Recognition of our social location in economic, national, and cultural realities.
- Evangelizing outsiders out of love rather than as a means to increase the size of the congregation.

Weaknesses

- It is reductionistic and simple, not considering the complexity of faith in a fallen world.
- It assumes that all modernism is bad and all postmodernism is good rather than critiquing each.
- In its attempt toward relativism, it fails to defend objective truth.
- The biblical scholarship in the movement is, at times, poor.
- It fails to use Scripture as the lens through which it embraces and adheres to tradition.

Carson's other concerns deal with

- the emergent emphasis on love without a balancing concern for the holiness of God—resulting in a weakened doctrine of sin
- ethical issues like homosexuality
- the existence of hell
- views on the atonement

Mark Liederbach and Alvin Reid[6] see the emergents as a convergence of existing streams of the Christian church. They trace the current expression of the emerging church to

- the Relevants—doctrinally conservative, but missionally innovative and contextual

- the Reconstructionists—using innovative structures and methods for the church, highly incarnational
- the Revisionists—reevaluating doctrine
- the Roamers—disenchanted with the conventional church, intrigued by the emergents

Liederbach and Reid compliment the emergents on their desire for vintage faith, missional emphasis, practice of the faith, communal authenticity, contextual relevance, and their recognition that we live in a postevangelical world.

Given this brief review, clearly there is no ironclad unity in the expression of the emerging church. It is not an organized institution with doctrinal statements, ethical codes, or administrative procedures. And it is not headquartered. Some emergents would wholeheartedly embrace some of the above characterizations while strongly rejecting others. Defining "emergent" is not like defining a given house or car. It means many things to many people.

If this is true for those who call themselves emergent, it is even truer for those who oppose the movement. Quite often, critics of the emerging church lump anything they do not like into the category of emergent. I suspect that much of the strident tone and emotion connected to this issue is more rooted in past church changes than in current expressions of the emerging church. The church has been waiting for a good enemy to oppose, an enemy that can be blamed for everything from jeans in the sanctuary to the removal of grandmother's organ.

And it may well be that the emergent movement is already passé, if not dead. Several writers, including Scott Daniels, have recognized that the discussion has moved on to other things. He suggests that the people keeping it alive are those who oppose it. As a university president, the only conversations I have had about the emergent church have come from responding to critics of the emergent church who believe that Christian universities have somehow gotten on the bandwagon of everything emergent. From my limited perspective, this has never happened. Daniels writes,

> Oh sure, there are still plenty of people talking and blogging about the EC. There are a few seminars still going on with either pro-emerging or anti-emerging overtones to them. But it is my prediction that one year from now even those lingering conversations will largely have faded into the distance. . . . The EC movement is essentially dead.[7]

Daniels suggests that the end of the movement may be explained by several factors.[8] When a movement gets marketed, it becomes a short-lived trend. With remarkable tongue-in-cheek humor he writes,

> In the increasingly market-oriented Christian world, people move on to the "next thing" in a hurry. Joe and Jane average Christian who started out praying the prayer of Jabez, only to then be filled with a fresh wind and fresh fire for a while, have wondered what Jesus would do, they have been purpose-driven for a season, they hung out in The Shack for a while, they've been emerging for a bit, and now it's time for whatever is next. So good luck finding a publisher who will print anything today with "emerging" in the title because, as the kids would say, "that's so 2009."[9]

Liberalism may also be part of the short shelf life of the emerging church. Again, in the words of Daniels,

> Unfortunately, many of the prophecies that the EC leaders were just early twentieth-century theological liberals in new clothing turned out to be true. I think self-proclaimed leaders of the EC went further theologically than those who were following could or would go. Personally, I think the mistake many of them made was when they left local church ministry and became travelling speakers focused on publishing careers. I am convinced that it is dangerous to be able to write or say whatever your publisher will let you get away with. In my own case I find it vitally important for me to stay accountable to the people I pastor and to remain under the authority of the denomination in which I'm ordained. That doesn't mean I don't appreciate those who keep the conversation lively at the boundaries of the faith. I do. But I think those discussions only stay grounded when they are ultimately tied to the historic Body of Christ in some tangible (and local) way.
>
> Particularly in the areas of atonement, justification, homosexuality, divine judgment, and the exclusivity of Christ, some of the most prominent EC leaders went further than those of us tied to historical communities of faith would or could go. I think that forms of deconstruction are healthy but only if they lead to new and better construction. I'm not sure some of the EC leaders ever got around to helping construct a faith—at least a faith that was still tied to the historical faith.[10]

Dead or alive, the conversation is still causing anxiety in many congregations. Maybe it is time for a civil discourse.

16

the EMERGING CHURCH
THE CHURCH IN CONVERSATION ABOUT THE CHURCH

We must not be quick to label the emerging church movement as an enemy. It is rooted in the same Scriptures, connected to the same historic roots, and hopeful for the redemption of all things. But the movement makes many people uncomfortable.

I am fifty-seven. Technology makes me uncomfortable. Just about the time I have mastered one cell phone, the university switches vendors and I am handed a new one, with more bells and whistles—and much smaller buttons and letters. I can't even read the face of the phone without glasses to magnify the print. And my fingers are chubby at the end, making it very hard for me to navigate the world on my iPhone. I know it does things I've never thought of doing on a phone, but it makes me rethink the way I operate.

The emerging church is forcing us to rethink the way we operate as the church of Jesus in the world. And in the words of my IT friends at the university, it will be good for us to do so. A little pain, as someone with a pebble in a shoe will attest, is a good motivator for us to do something.

So what do we do?

Modern vs. Postmodern

It is time for many of us to stop castigating anything that goes under the label "postmodern" and educate ourselves on the ways the world is changing. The next time you hear the word, don't scowl. Say, "I'm not sure I understand what 'postmodern' means. Would you explain to me what you mean by it?" All that is postmodern is not bad. The postmodern world is similar in many ways to New Testament days as the gospel went into a pluralistic society. At the same time, all that was/is modern is not bad. The significant contributions of modern science, medical research, and historical criticism cannot be denied. Moderns and postmoderns now occupy the same time and space. It is not a war to see which side wins, but rather two different ways of thinking. A thoughtful Christian will seek to comprehend the positives and negatives of each.

The Grandchildren of the Church

In many ways, the emerging Christians are doing what our oldest members grew up doing—taking care of the poor, living simply, and radically loving the neighbor. They are willing to listen to history—something baby boomers were never accused of. They are more comfortable in the world of the immigrants that came to America from everywhere, forming communities and cities. They are more generationally sensitive than the megawatt, decibel-blasting stage performers of my generation. They do not embrace a narrow selection of music but are open to the expressions of the ages. They will even ask someone over fifty to sing again in church. If we show these emerging Christians the door, we are saying good-bye to the grandchildren of the church.

Worshipping Worship

Worship styles will come and go. To defend a favorite worship style is to misunderstand worship at its core. Worship is about God. If our worship is about our favorite style, it is not about God—it is about us. Enough with the worship wars. Let's participate in the quest for meaningful ways to experience the presence of God who longs to be among us. Some churches will find old hymns, organs, testimony services, and altar calls meaningful. Others will find art, new songs, and drama meaningful. The multigenerational church will find some of each. The primary issue is not style, but story. As long as our worship is centered in the story of the God who is known as Father, Son, and Spirit, we are on the same page, though singing in different locations.[1] The worship of God's people is as diverse as the books of the Bible, yet the same God is present in all.

Missional Focus

The emerging Christians are right about missional focus. The church, for far too long, has been more interested in its seating capacity than in its sending capacity. Until the church of Jesus gets outside its walls and practices social justice, compassion, and neighbor-love, we are not the church of Jesus. This move is not original with emerging Christians. Pastors have been saying this most of my lifetime. Megachurch growth methods have subtly taught us to view people as part of our growth strategy rather than persons for whom Christ died. Denominational ladder climbing has rewarded pastors who pack pews. Being a faithful pastor in a dying community or a small congregation of needy people is rarely celebrated. While it is true that healthy bodies grow, it is also true that sick ones need tending.

I remember a decisive moment in one of my pastorates. I was urging our people to get out beyond the church walls into the community to reach the lost—a worthy calling. There was resistance. Many in the congregation were accustomed to church being mostly about them, and the role of the pastor being to serve them. I was irked somewhat. The octane in a few of my sermons crossed the line in reminding these insiders that Jesus loved sinners and so should they. One day while grousing to God about these recalcitrant members, God reminded me in simple words, "I love found people too."

The missional church is motivated to go into the world, but it is also given to the care and tending of those who are already within the community. When love, rather than church growth, drives both of these endeavors, the church is healthy.

Systematic and Narrative Theology

The move from modernism to postmodernism is often described as a move from logical explanations to storytelling. That is partly true. The modern scientific method knew how to dissect anything down to its smallest components, but it was helpless to declare the meaning of the relationship of the parts or the purpose of the greater whole. It was a method of logic, building blocks, outlines, and Tinkertoy constructs. Postmodernism seeks meaning in the story of a person and peoples. Could it be that each has its place, that neither is wrong or right, but that both are necessary for good thinking? Doctrine is strongest when it can be clearly stated systematically and narratively. In the Wesleyan way, Scripture is interpreted through the lens of tradition, reason, and experience. One finds plenty of room for orderly linear thinking and compelling story.

Political Correctness

The emerging Christians are critiquing our tendency as denominations to crawl in bed with political parties. See the chapter on religion and politics for the larger discussion on this issue. The kingdom of God cannot be co-opted. It cannot be subsumed by a political party and loses its soul if it seeks to identify with one. Our political world needs open discussion on complex ethical issues, and the church could be the place where charitable discourse once again finds a home. Churches should be quick to declare that party affiliation is not a plank in the platform of church membership, implied or spoken.

The emergents are also right to call for caution about nationalism in the church. Given the makeup of our cities, it is possible to have people from many nations and languages worshipping in the same congregation. We are responsible to pray for our government leaders but not to make the church the haven of our national aspirations. The kingdom of God supersedes all other memberships and citizenships.

The College and the Seminary

Denominations have vested interests in colleges and seminaries. These are places where God-called servants do their ministry by helping the church think, by analyzing the current culture, and by forming the next generation of Christian leaders. For all congregations to "go local" and cease their support of Christian seminaries and colleges is to participate in the loss of the most formative segment of the theological future. Many of the young scholars of the emerging church movement graduated from Christian universities. The people who have the capacity to correct, instruct, and critique them are their former professors. The generations of Christian scholars keep in touch through these institutions. As evil as these institutions can become, they are essential as keepers of the faith, historians of Christian doctrine, and gathering places for the training of the next generation. If the church has no space dedicated to asking the hard questions in the context of its best thinkers, it is doomed. If denominations cannot identify, support, and hold accountable great scholars, where will they emerge, who will they be indebted to, and who will they serve?

I realize that many denominations have already "lost" their colleges. These schools began as servants to the church but now are independent of the church that formed them. It appears that faith and learning have a hard time holding hands over the long haul. I am privileged to serve a university that not only remains accountable to its founding faith and church but also aggressively looks for ways to serve that church and the world. When a university becomes a smorgasbord of religious convictions and doctrines, we lose the compelling narrative of a Wesleyan, Reformed, or Catholic way of thinking. If the emerging church dismantles our learning centers even further by the loss of denominational congregations, we will lose an important piece of our identity as the people of God in the world.

It is a given that the dividing line on many of the issues addressed in this book is education. Scholars see things differently. Fundamentalism is rooted in an opposition to higher criticism and scientific exploration. Folk theology operates best where no challenge is presented to counter its assumptions. This is not to say that the scholars are always right, or that they are always wrong. I anticipate difficult days ahead for scholarly servants who seek to remain faithful while serving the church. If the jihadic way of thinking becomes the norm, the educated will need to check their brains at the door to participate in the local church. This will be a sad day for both. My hopes rest in a common unifying reality—the Christ "who became for us wisdom from God, and righteousness and sanctification and redemption, in order that, as it is written, 'Let the one who boasts, boast in the Lord'" (1 Cor. 1:30).

Denominations

Denominations are on the decline in the United States. It is time for us to discuss anew the positives and negatives of denominations. I believe the negative case includes issues like hierarchies, power structures, self-preservation over mission, and operating the church on a business model. I do not know of any denomination that has not struggled with these issues. It is good and right for us to discuss the ways that our own denomination has been affected by modern assumptions, a materialistic culture, and power-driven business models.

On the other hand, there is a positive case to be made for compassionate and evangelistic missions of a size that can be sustained only by the joint commitment of the churches of a denomination. For every local congregation to attack HIV in Africa would be a gross waste of resources that could be combined for much stronger impact.

The church I pastored from 1991 to 2005 had two timely opportunities to get involved in global issues. Following the genocide in Rwanda, we financed five pioneer missionary families to Rwanda, built a church in the capitol city of Kigali (the first new congregation in the city with Hutus and Tutsis worshipping together), and built another twelve rural churches. Following the invasion of Iraq, we adopted and supported a church in Baghdad. Our congregation continues support to this church to this day. Belonging to a denomination was critical to our success in these projects. As a local congregation, we could never have made this impact. However, in our local community, we established an independent 501(c)(3) nonprofit organization to care for the poor, provide medical care, and love the neighbor. We did not need a denomination to do this. It is possible to embrace denominational initiatives without sacrificing local ministry.

Brian McLaren, a leader in the emerging church movement, has listed seven things denominations do well.[2]

1. "Embody an ethos." Denominations create and preserve a brand of Christian faith that is recognizable and consistent.
2. "Conserve treasures." These include "doctrines, memories, and virtues."
3. "Support relationships." "They help people find local churches" and connect people across generations in diverse locations.
4. "Protect physical assets." They care for "buildings, universities, [and] publications."
5. "Protect and preserve human assets." They provide "pensions, insurance, and professional development."
6. "See and solve problems." Denominations are able to amass resources to address major issues of concern.
7. "Create policies." They establish structures for dealing with repeated situations and bring the experience of repetition to the table to address how to act and react.

McLaren, a hero of many emergents, is quick to recognize the value in denominations but also offers a challenge. Denominations must focus on new as well as old treasures. They should move beyond supporting existing relationships to expanding the connections between the various bodies so that cross-denominational learning and partnership can occur. Denominations should strategically leverage their massive assets for the work of the kingdom, not the preservation of the denomination.

History tells us that no movement continues for long without some level of institutional development. Movements become organizations that over time grow into institutions. If the emerging church is around fifty years from now, it will probably be a headquartered association with recognized spokespersons, recognized practices, preferred universities, and favorite authors. It already has some of these.

17

the EMERGING CHURCH COMING TO A TOWN NEAR YOU

Is the model of Christlike holiness best served by a church that fights or a church that loves? Where is Christian maturity at work—in an arrogant dismissal of emerging church thinking or a welcomed conversation where the issues are honestly discussed? What is the Christian way to deal with emerging Christians—to smear them on a Web site, taking their comments out of context, or to pick up the phone and have a conversation, even offering to host them in our homes for an extended visit in hopes of mutual understanding and respect?

Recently, I corresponded with a pastor whose story saddens me. I have changed the names and locations to disguise his identity, but the story is true. I will let him tell the story via letters.

Dan,

I hope things are going well for you on the hilltop. I miss the southeast and the occasional visit to Trevecca living in the south afforded me.

I have read your interchange with the opponents of the emerging church. I thought your responses to them were gracious, thoughtful, direct, biblical, and transparent.

Just so you know, my church of 115 is now a fellowship of 75. I have attackers of the emerging church to thank for that. If you're ever interested in a worst-case scenario for what happens when this stuff takes root in the hearts of rigid fundamentalists, give me a call. Honestly, I didn't mind pastoring fundamentalists. They're great tithers (smiley face), and pragmatically, most conversations can be settled with, "Because the Bible says so"—although, I don't think I've actually ever said that. As our historians and theologians have pointed out, the church has always had these folks under our umbrella. This anti-emergent rhetoric is giving them the ammunition to poke holes in our broad umbrella of Wesleyan theology. When they cannot poke holes in it any longer, they ultimately are going to leave.

[Six] months ago, my problem started when I got an e-mail from someone that had one sentence in it, "Pastor, what do you think of the Emergent Church?" Knowing the stir that this issue was causing, I gave a balanced response. Balanced . . . not good enough. I was quickly labeled an emergent, and after not allowing a meeting for the sole purpose of distributing their material, the witch hunt was on.

Things got ugly, mainly because I refused to engage in the debate. I usually responded with, "That's something you should ask our denominational leaders," or "We don't do prayer labyrinths at our church, so that's not my fight." I found so much of this to be an absolute drain on my time and the work of ministry to which I had been called.

The endgame for these folks was pulling away from our church. They started their own church in Podunk Holler made up entirely of former First Church folks. About 30 of them meet at a funeral home chapel. The scheme to do so was largely hatched in a Sunday school class . . . probably during church . . . I'll never really know . . . and at this point, it's better that I don't dwell on it.

The worst is behind me . . . praise God. My faith will survive this, thanks in part to a wonderful church family (those that remained), a wonderful district superintendent, and the prayers of many loving friends.

Like I said, I didn't mind serving fundamentalists, and things are a lot more "fun" now that they are gone. The last six weeks of services have been anointed, and we are reaching new people that the Lord is dumping in our lap. There is a spirit of unity and everyone that remains at First wants to see the mission of the church accomplished. Interesting that the anti-emergent folks did in six months, what sixteen years of pastors before me could not.

Dan, I've attached a letter that I contemplated sending to those who left my church. It sums up my thoughts on the anti-emergent conversation. Some of what I included is indebted to David Felter[1] (I have appreciated his stand). As of today, I finally resolved to NOT send this letter. I'm just tired of fighting, and perhaps this letter was my way of "wielding the sword." I just couldn't take a chance of causing more hurt, even though I have the best of intentions.

I share this with you just so you know what this looks like in the trenches. I want my experience to help other pastors who are in the same boat. If you receive calls or e-mails from anyone going through the same thing, please don't hesitate to send them my way. I'd love to encourage them and let them know what life looks like on the other side.

Dan, you are loved and appreciated. Keep up the good work.

Pastor Matthew

He composed the following as a cathartic act but did not send it. But then, maybe he did.

April 3, 2010

Dear Friends,

It is unfortunate that you no longer worship at First Church. The last few months have been painful for me as a pastor. I have heard stories of your pain as well. Many of us have wounds that will never heal. We may ignore or forget about them in time, but true healing can never happen until Christ's disciples look one another in the face and say, "I'm sorry."

Let me be the first to express this sentiment. I am sorry and do sincerely apologize for any lack of judgment, discernment, or pastoral care that you may attribute to me. I'm not sure what I could have done six months ago to prevent your departure from this body of believers. However, if I could have done anything to prevent this that did not compromise who I am as an ordained elder in the church, I would have done so.

With all pastoral sincerity and care may I also express how division in the body of believers is wrong. Offering rebuke is not enjoyable and against my nature, but I would be doing you a disservice were I to withhold this from you. How many scriptures emphasize the unity of God's people? Here are but a few:

> My prayer is not for them alone. I pray also for those who will believe in me through their message, that all of them may be one, Father, just as you are in me and I am in you *(John 17:20-21*a, *NIV).*
>
> There are six things the LORD hates, seven that are detestable to him: haughty eyes, a lying tongue, hands that shed innocent blood, a heart that devises wicked schemes, feet that are quick to rush into evil, a false witness who pours out lies and a man who stirs up dissension among brothers *(Prov. 6:16-19, NIV).*
>
> As a prisoner for the Lord, then, I urge you to live a life worthy of the calling you have received. Be completely humble and gentle; be patient, bearing with one another in love. Make every effort to keep the unity of the Spirit through the bond of peace. There is one body and one Spirit—just as you were called to one hope when you were called—one Lord, one faith, one baptism; one God and Father of all, who is over all and through all and in all *(Eph. 4:1-6, NIV).*

I have been told the decision to leave First Church may not have been about our local church, but more about our denomination. However, this decision is shortsighted, lacks kingdom perspective, is oblivious to the feelings of others, and is ultimately driven by personal agendas.

As you move forward in this new venture, I have to remind you that the actions that led to the split of our church and the gospel of Jesus Christ are incompatible. Surely, you must have been aware of the pain and confusion that would be left in the wake of such action. What do you intend to accomplish by this? How does the splitting of First Church accomplish God's kingdom purposes in our city? Is this how God has chosen to reach people estranged from him? Yes, God works in mysterious ways, but he does not work in ways contrary to that which he has revealed in Scripture. Whatever good comes from the schism created by your actions will not stem from God's divine plan, but rather by his gracious redemption in spite of your actions.

Friends, the church is in a culture that is rapidly changing. Every church and denomination finds itself in an age of unparalleled cultural shifts. What has come to be referred to as the "emerging church" is the attempt by some to make the gospel relevant in the midst of these changes. These attempts have been successful at times, and at other times they have been disastrous. I share some of the concerns that you have.

For instance, there is no doubt that some in the "emerging church" have minimized the importance of the Holy Scriptures. In an attempt to be relevant to a culture with no absolute truth, some have devalued the only absolute we have. This is an error in judgment. I, too, am concerned about this.

As the established church, how shall we now respond to this error? Perhaps we should ask ourselves, "How would Jesus respond?" Would Jesus start a Web site that attacked other Christians? Would Jesus condemn these attempts as heresy and threaten to cut them off from fellowship? Would Jesus use the venue of a worship service to distribute material that ultimately divides the people of God?

It's true that Jesus made a whip of cords, overturned the tables of the money changers, and cleared the temple. It's also true that Jesus said, "I did not come to bring peace, but a sword" (Matt. 10:34, NIV). Jesus was no stranger to extreme methods and was anything but conventional. However, the overwhelming witness of the Bible clearly demonstrates the call to Christlikeness has less to do with clearing temples and wielding swords and more to do with loving our neighbor and our enemy with unconditional love . . . especially when we disagree.

Jesus' betrayal and arrest is told in similar detail by all four evangelists. Here is Luke's account:

> While he was still speaking a crowd came up, and the man who was called Judas, one of the Twelve, was leading them. He approached Jesus to kiss him, but Jesus asked him, "Judas, are you betraying the Son of Man with a kiss?" When Jesus' followers saw what was going to happen, they said, "Lord, should we strike with our swords?" And one of them struck the servant of the high priest, cutting off his right ear. But Jesus answered, "No more of this!" And he touched the man's ear and healed him *(Luke 22:47-51, NIV).*

The Garden of Gethsemane is not too far from where the church finds itself today. Here we are in the midst of cultural change, often hostile to the church. The response to this change is multifaceted. It is filled with good intentions but is at times an emerging theological error. We look to our Savior and ask if we should strike with our swords.

No response.

Surely our Lord does not desire for us to sit here and do nothing while everything we have worked for so hard seems in danger of being lost. We take matters into our own hands, wielding the sword and cutting off ears. At a time when listening is needed more than talking, we close our ears to that which is foreign to us and cut off the ears of those whose response to cultural change makes us uncomfortable.

Finally, our Lord speaks, "No more of this!" We wait for him to say the word and call down fire upon his enemies. What he does next surprises everyone. He extends his hands and heals the ears of his enemies. Through the healing touch of Christ we are able to listen to one another again.

Christ's actions toward those who oppose him, misunderstand him, reject him, and seek to destroy him teach us all a lesson. Perhaps, we should leave the wielding of the sword to Christ. Let's allow him to be the one who overturns the tables and drives the money changers from his house.

Who is really qualified, other than our Lord, to purge his Church? Has God really appointed some to be prophets, some to be apostles, some to be evangelists, and some to be his theology police? The end of scripture reveals that the Church Triumphant will be gathered by Christ himself. He will not need my help or your help in finding his Bride.

I'm not sure what the future of your new "Wesleyan congregation" is. However, if you truly desire to align yourself with the thought and practice of John Wesley, there are some things you need to understand about who he was. The spiritual revival that took place during Wesley's day was not ignited because John Wesley convinced the world to get their theology straight. The 1700s were filled with just as many competing ideas about God as we have today. John Wesley never wrote a systematic theology. He never sat down and organized an orderly account of all the Bible teaches about God, humanity, sin, and salvation. All we have from Wesley is pastoral in nature. It was theology and biblical exposition done within an ever-changing context, one that emerged out of the needs of the people.

The need for Christian unity was essential to what John Wesley was trying to accomplish as evidenced from this excerpt from one of his sermons—"Catholic Spirit." Nothing Wesley said is as salient to the situation at First Church and to the larger anti-emergent conversation as this:

> I dare not, therefore, presume to impose my mode of worship on any other. I believe it is truly primitive and apostolic. But my belief is no rule for another. I ask not, therefore, of him with whom I would unite in love, "Are you of my church, of my congregation? Do you receive the same form of church government, and allow the same church of-

ficers, with me? Do you join in the same form of prayer by which I worship God?"

I inquire not, "Do you receive the Lord's supper in the same posture and manner that I do?" Nor do I inquire whether, in the administration of baptism, you agree with me in admitting sureties for the baptized, in the manner of administering it, or the age of those to whom it should be administered. I do not even ask of you (as clear as I am in my own mind) whether you allow baptism and the Lord's Supper at all. Let all these things stand by. We will talk of them, if need be, at a more convenient season. My only question at present is this, "Is your heart right, as my heart is with your heart?"

. . . The first thing implied is this: Is your heart right with God? Do you believe his being and his perfections, his eternity, immensity, wisdom, power, his justice, mercy, and truth? Do you believe that he now "upholds all things by the word of his power," and that he governs even the most minute, even the most noxious, to his own glory and the good of them that love him? Have you a divine evidence, a supernatural conviction, of the things of God? Do you "walk by faith not by sight," looking not at temporal things but things eternal?

Do you believe in the Lord Jesus Christ, "God over all, blessed for ever?" Is he revealed in your soul? Do you know Jesus Christ and him crucified? Does he dwell in you and you in him? Is he formed in your heart by faith? Having absolutely renounced all your own works, your own righteousness, have you submitted yourself unto the righteousness of God, which is by faith in Christ Jesus? Are you "found in him, not having your own righteousness, but the righteousness which is by faith?" And are you, through him, "fighting the good fight of faith, and laying hold of eternal life?"

. . . If it be, give me your hand. I do not mean, "Be of my opinion." You need not. I do not expect or desire it. Neither do I mean, "I will be of your opinion." I cannot, it does not depend on my choice. I can no more think, than I can see or hear, as I will. Keep your opinion and I will keep mine, and that as steadily as ever. You need not even endeavor to come over to me, or bring me over to you. I do not desire you to dispute those points, or to hear or speak one word concerning them. Leave all opinions alone on one side and the other: only give me your hand.[2]

That's all I have ever asked of anyone under my pastoral care. You don't have to "be of my opinion." It's unfortunate—that which I have never asked of anyone has been required of me, it has been required of the sheep under my care, and it is being demanded of the church—that we be of your opinion or else. Such a congruence of opinions is idealistic and impossible.

Therefore, the only test Wesley presents for those who labor for the gospel is simple and broad in its scope, "Do you know Jesus Christ and him crucified? Does he dwell in you and you in him?" If this is your heart, if this is who you are, if this is who God's Holy Spirit is calling you to be, then give me your hand.

Until He's Finished,
Pastor Matthew

Friends, we have much more to lose for the sake of Christ's church by unholy discourse and enemy making than by embracing emerging Christians as brothers and sisters. While there are needed corrections in some emerging theologies, we need not fear the conversation, unless, of course, we fear that we may also be changed. And if we fear being changed, we will never experience sanctification, which is ultimately about a lifelong transformation into the image and likeness of Jesus.

section *3*

THE MORE EXCELLENT WAY

The theology of holy love has as much to lose from a divisive, arrogant spirit as from the positions we end up with. It may be that we win the verbal spar, the war of castigation, the battle for minds, the political election—and lose the peace that characterizes Christ. And while we duke it out, a generation has left the church in hopes of finding an honest, mature conversation to join.

This reality has become the call of my life—to live among young thinkers in hopes of instilling a way of conversing that honors God, deals with life, is shaped by Scripture, and forms a generation of holy leaders who have the courage to live and think like the kingdom—people of God rather than the people of the kingdoms of the world.

18

TABLE TALK *with* TRINITY

My friend Dean Blevins presented a paper at Trevecca Nazarene University titled "Global Pedagogy: A Table Conversation." He discussed three current ways of teaching, conversing with, and shaping the coming generations.

The first, "McWorld,"[1] is the attempt to standardize culture through consumption of goods. Companies portray their products as generic, but they contain cultural and theological assumptions. Marketing these goods persuasively convinces people that the quality of their life is rooted in the consumption of these goods. Images and slogans reduce persons to passive consumers. The assumption is "one size fits all." There is only one way to think about life and one product that delivers that life to the willing consumers.

The second pedagogy, "Jihad," is the logical reaction to McWorld. This extreme term accurately describes various, often violent, responses. The political implications of jihad are horrendous internationally. Jihad forms communities through coercion. The mind is shaped to react to outside influence, rejecting positive contributions, and restricting reflection and critique. Jihad refuses diversity and adopts a peculiar and often intimidating fundamentalism by insisting on a particular way of viewing the world. Teachers compel students to adopt one vision while trivializing or attacking other approaches.

The church lives in a world being shaped by both ways of forming communities. The American church, rampantly consumerist, has clawed its way to respectability on the cultural stage by its growing ability to outsing, outentertain, outclass, outbuild, outearn the world. We have effectively learned to "outworld the world." When our Christian brother wins the Super Bowl, American Idol, or a Grammy, we have arrived. We have now tasted the world's goods at the highest level. Our "stars" become the teachers of our young as they are encouraged to go and do likewise.

But when we cannot get the world to cooperate with our attempt to rule from the consumerist perch, we take a page from the jihadists and attack the enemy with a violence of words and characterizations that destroy. The church is schizophrenic, not knowing whether to compete on the global platform for the prize or huddle in fearful safety as we condemn the infidels to hell for not agreeing with us.

But there is a third possibility—"Table Conversation." This theological metaphor suggests that we are a family gathered around a common meal. Our meal is rooted in the sacrament of Communion, reminding us of the story of Jesus. He came that we might be one as he is one with the Father and Spirit. We are invited into the love that exists among Trinity and are shaped by the kind of conversation that might occur among Trinity. Many found the novel *The Shack* to be enlightening as it reminded us of the kind of meal that Trinity might have—self-emptying love, other-affirming openness, unity within diversity. As we eat at this table, we are shaped into a particular family of God.

This family finds its identity, not in what it consumes or in what it labels enemy, but in the ways of Trinity. These bonds are not forged by common commodities or coercion but by our transforming vision of God. We are not clones or dittoheads or robots. We are brothers and sisters related to each other in Christ. We are not a hate-filled army unified in the overthrow of the enemy but responsible stewards and witnesses who are taught to love the enemy like God loves the enemy. When we eat together at the Lord's Table, we do this in remembrance of him. We relive the life, death, and resurrection of Jesus through our formation as a Jesus-like community. When we talk at the table, we are practicing the love that flows within the family of Trinity. When we leave the table, we are being given to the world for God's purposes, going into it as God has already gone into it—to bless. As we go, we are charged with "seeing God" in the poor, the sick, the imprisoned. We view the world through the lens of servant, not consumer or coercer. We become the presence of God, the body of Christ, as we are the location of the activity of God. I am convinced that our best hope of a charitable discourse, of having a holy conversation, is to recover our identity as the people of Trinity. But we have a major issue with our view of ourselves as individuals.

Our culture identifies a person as a separate individual with an identifiable body, a recognizable face, and distinguishing characteristics. In other words, we identify ourselves as separate skin-sacks of blood and bones.[2]

If God is "three persons, blessed Trinity,"[3] can we do with God what we can do with three persons? Can we separate God? Put Father in one room, Jesus in another, and the Spirit somewhere else? Can we get them to disagree? Can one vote Democrat, one Republican, and one Independent? Can they divorce? Can we find characteristics true of one but not of the other two?

Sure, these are silly questions. But maybe not as silly as some of our folk theology about God. Have you heard the one about the Father sitting miffed in heaven, ticked off with what we've done to his creation, and poor Jesus running around earth trying to placate the Father so he'd love us again? Or the one about getting Jesus when I was saved but getting the Holy Spirit when I was sanctified? (Maybe this suggests a third work of grace in which we receive the Father!)

If we think of God as we think of persons, we can think silly things. But maybe our definition of "person" is all wrong. In the Bible a person is identified not by his or her separateness from others but by a connection to others. An Israelite is a son or daughter of Abraham. Saul is named as one who belongs to the tribe of Benjamin. Covenants unite people and give them their identity. Personhood is not our radical difference from each other but our radical belonging to each other.

And where did we learn this? By looking into the face of God. God cannot be divided into three pieces that make sense alone. When we say "God," we mean Father, Son, and Spirit. It is impossible to explain what any one of the three does without reference to the other two. God is inseparable. We would not know God as Father apart from Jesus revealing this to us. God is rarely spoken of as "Father" in the Old Testament. It is Jesus who teaches us to pray "Our Father." The Spirit is the breath of God who creates and resurrects. Into the dark, formless chaos God breathes. Into the dead body of Jesus, God breathes. We call this the Holy Spirit. Jesus as Risen Lord is incomprehensible apart from the Holy Breath of God, the Spirit. The Father who creates sends the Son who redeems through the Spirit who sanctifies us into the union that exists as Father, Son, and Spirit.

Have you ever seen three children in a circle, holding hands, going round and round in an ecstasy of laughter, love, rhythm, and unity? This is a picture of Trinity. That there are three means that a decision has been made to be inclusive. Movement depends on paying attention to the others. Each follows in step. No one leads. The joy on each face is a reflection of the joy on the other two. Life and energy exist in the center of the circle.

Another way of thinking about the relationship called Trinity is to think of beautiful music. The notes derive their beauty from their relationship to other notes in the music. To separate the notes and examine each one individually is to massacre the composition and miss the inherent beauty. God is a rhythmic relationship of love, beauty, and grace.

This idea of God as a circle dance is not original. It is very old. *Perichoresis* is the technical term for circle dance. We can learn charitable discourse from this image of God.

Conversation is possible because it is already going on in the center of the circle. The idea that conversation begins when we come together to hash out an issue is misinformed. Conversation is already going on among Father, Son, and Spirit. The table simply reminds us that we are graciously invited into the fellowship known as Trinity. God has extended the invitation in the name of Jesus. We step into a stream of holy talk that started before the world was formed. We are latecomers. And lest we think that we have discovered something new, we need to remember that creation itself flows from the center of this circle dance.

One Wednesday night, we divided our congregation into three groups and sang in a round. We were singing, "Father, I Adore You," with separate lines for Jesus and the Holy Spirit.

Our sanctuary extended in three directions, all facing the center pulpit. As people sang, they were actually looking at each other. It was a beautiful moment as different words rose and fell in the mixture of sounds. We were singing three different lines at one time, but one song. It was godly. This was not something we created. We were being drawn into the circle dance of God, where Father, Son, and Spirit move in perfect rhythm, singing to each other the song of self-emptying adoration. Imagine it. The Father sings his adoration to Jesus, and Jesus sings at the same time his adoration back to the Father.

Jesus is offering himself to God as a sacrifice for our sins. He is offering his perfect obedience on our behalf. And both Father and Son sing love to the Spirit who proceeds from them to create and resurrect the world and its creatures.

God is singing an eternal round of love, adoration, life, and self-emptying grace. And we are invited into this circle.

Holy conversation is not something we do for God. It is the gift of God to people who have no invitation to the dance of life. We were sitting at home, dead, without a lover, and the-Father-in-Christ-through-the-Spirit invited us to dance. We experience rhythm and love and unity that we didn't create. The fact that we can converse at the table of God is sheer grace.

Belonging at this table is not dependent on any litmus test of political conviction, scientific theory, gender, sexual orientation, or philosophical worldview. It hinges on being invited by the God who comes to live in his cosmic temple, who dies in time and history on our behalf, and who is active in the risen Christ by the power of the Spirit making all things new.

Am I suggesting that it doesn't matter how we live? That we can think whatever we want and be included at the table as members of the family? No, it doesn't mean that at all. It means that our lives are being shaped by the conversation at the table into the likeness of Jesus.

> I appeal to you therefore, brothers and sisters, by the mercies of God, to present your bodies as a living sacrifice, holy and acceptable to God, which is your spiritual worship. Do not be conformed to this world, but be transformed by the renewing of your minds, so that you may discern what is the will of God—what is good and acceptable and perfect *(Rom. 12:1-2).*

If we can change our understanding of "person" from "an individual disconnected from others," to "one defined by belonging to a common story and people," we have a good chance of having a charitable discourse on divisive topics. We will become a reflection of Trinity.

But this is a tall order. Our cultural definition of "person" is

- I am an individual.
- I am distinguishable from you.
- I have a social security number that is different from yours.
- I exist in this identifiable skin-sack.

- I make choices in line with my ruling desires.
- I enter relationships that are meaningful to me.
- I seek out experiences that are relevant to me.
- I have limited time and do not want to waste it on uninteresting people.
- I am not obligated to you unless I choose to be, and you have no right to expect anything from me unless I give you that right.
- I choose my politics.
- I decide whether or not women can preach.
- I decide my sexual ethics, my opinion about homosexuality, my theory of creation.
- I am responsible for myself.

This is the dominant theology of our culture regarding humans. There is a good label for this person. Call him or her a *consumer*. This individual is reaching out into the world, taking things into himself or herself. This person consumes experiences, people, and things. And this person decides what to do with those who are "different" by practicing jihad.

By stark contrast, the biblical definition of "person" would be

- I am a child of God.
- I belong to the people of God by baptism.
- I exist as a body in a body.
- I take interest in the lives of my brothers and sisters. Some are energizing, some are draining.
- I am obligated. People have the right to expect certain things of me in light of the covenant that exists between us.
- I seek to be faithful to them.
- I cannot think of myself apart from the body of Christ.
- I am given the mind of Christ regarding women in ministry, sexual practices, concern for the effect of alcohol on the neighbor, homosexuals, differing theories of the origin of creation, the emerging church.
- I learn to think about these things at the table as Trinity guides the body in conversation.
- I am a new creation.

This is the dominant theology of Scripture regarding humans. There is a good label for this person. Call him or her a *member*. This individual belongs to all who are in Christ and views the world through this lens.

When you think "member," think biologically, such as a family member or a member of the human body—an arm, a leg, a neck. We find that word in the Bible:

> For as in one body we have many *members*, and not all the *members* have the same function, so we, who are many, are one body in Christ, and individually we are *members* one of another *(Rom. 12:4-5, emphasis added).*

———

> So then you are no longer strangers and aliens, but you are citizens with the saints and also *members* of the household of God, built upon the foundation of the apostles and prophets, with Christ Jesus himself as the cornerstone. In him the whole structure is joined together and grows into a holy temple in the Lord; in whom you also are built together spiritually into a dwelling place for God *(Eph. 2:19-22, emphasis added).*

———

> So then, putting away falsehood, let all of us speak the truth to our neighbors, for we are *members* of one another *(Eph. 4:25, emphasis added).*

Being a member of the body of Christ shapes our involvement with each other. We gather at the table of God because this is where our identity is rooted. This is our family—when the issues are difficult, when science frightens us, when discourse is strained, when we don't understand. We stay at the table because we are *members,* not *consumers.* Consumers check out the product (position on divisive issue) and determine whether they wish to consume it (stay) or not (leave). Members just show up and stay because they belong.

This places new weight on the meaning and practice of Communion. We are at the table together. Communion is not an intimate dinner for two—just Jesus and me; just Jesus and you. It is the meal that was cooked up in the middle of a circle dance. The aroma is compelling. We don't get our food and go eat under a tree. We sit down at the table with everyone else and share in the fellowship created by Father, Son, and Spirit. We look each other in the face and remember that we belong to each other in Christ. The Spirit is at work in the meal sanctifying us together as one.

This places new weight on the meaning and practice of baptism into the body of Jesus. In baptism, we are given a new identity. We now have the right to expect things of each other. We are bound together in ways we cannot ignore without damage to the body.

This places new weight on church membership. We ought to make it more meaningful than a name in a book. It is a person's decision to be identified with the visible people of God. They are joining the family as responsible servants and workers. They have the right to expect things of us, and we of them. We're asking far more than agreement with doctrine and ethics. We're asking them to understand that we actually belong to each other.

This places new weight on our worship gatherings. We are not consumers looking for a praise and worship pick-me-up. We are the body of Christ, gathered in his name, participating as one in a circle dance of loving grace.

This places new weight on our life of prayer. We may pray alone, but even private devotions do not isolate us from the body. We are praying to "*Our* Father in heaven." We are remembering each other before God. We are learning to love as God loves. Maybe this is why we are to pray for those who persecute us, say bad things about us, and try to make us the enemy. In prayer, they belong to us in the presence of Trinity. If we can hold them before a God of love, maybe we can converse in charity.

19

good OLD-FASHIONED INDIVIDUAL RESPONSIBILITY

Having said such wonderful things about our corporate identity, our bodyness, our being members of one another, we must now state the obvious. We can only experience this as individuals. The pendulum may have swung too far in the direction of corporate identity, excusing us from personal responsibility within community. The pendulum swing is understandable. As rugged American individuals with a John Wayne/Rambo/superhero mentality, we needed the correction of communal membership. But now, we may need to recover some of the value of standing on our own two feet and accepting responsibility for what we say and do.

Groupthink has taken over. Repeating the racial, sexual, or political slurs that dismiss a person or idea is a highly corporate act. We have bought into the thinking of others without ever asking the hard questions, without running it through the grid of Scripture, doctrinal/ethical tradition, reason, and human experience. We become dittoheads of someone else's making. Our corporate identity makes us uncorrectable.

In a previous congregation, our leaders decided to take on the task of defining the biblical behavior to be practiced when there was a division in the church. We wished to instruct our people, as members of the body of Christ *and* as responsible individuals in that body, about scriptural practices in a biblically functioning community. The question before us was, "How will our church deal with divisive issues?" The process of writing the statement was as formative as the finished paper. Leaders were engaged in studying the Scriptures and defining the behaviors suggested for the people of God. The form of the statement is somewhat linear and heavy on scripture quotations, often without accompanying explanations of the context of those scriptures, but this was the final form of the paper. It served the congregation well and gave us a model to follow.

The Issue

As we, the body of Christ, seek to become fully devoted followers of our Lord, it is important that we consider how we will handle divisive issues in our community. Since we represent diverse sociological, economic, political, and educational backgrounds, it is a given that we will bring varied opinions and practices into this community of faith. We welcome the diversity and recognize it as a sign that the church is not a gathering of the same kind of people. The gospel is penetrating culture and redeeming individuals from all sectors of society. Differing opinions are a positive, not a negative. We seek to see each person through the eyes of Jesus, knowing that he gave his life for each one and that God has no favorites in his kingdom. Recognizing that disagreements, discord, and disunity will surface within the church, it is imperative that our community deal with these in a way that pleases God.

The Bible provides a standard by which we should live. John 13:35 admonishes us to let love be our identifying characteristic. "By this all men will know that you are my disciples, if you love one another" (NIV). Love is the overarching principle in dealing with divisiveness. We will not allow injury to the body of Christ by excusing the sins of a brother or sister. Yet we must be tolerant in matters where the issue is not of doctrinal or ethical value. Phineas F. Bresee, founder of the Church of the Nazarene, said, "In essentials, unity; in nonessentials, liberty; in all things, charity."

In the Bible, acceptable and nonacceptable behavior patterns are clearly set forth. As to the positive side of the godly life, "the fruit of the Spirit is love, joy, peace, patience, kindness, goodness, faithfulness, gentleness and self-control" (Gal. 5:22-23, NIV). Unhealthy behaviors are also listed. "Now the works of the flesh are obvious: fornication, impurity, licentiousness, idolatry, sorcery, enmities, strife, jealousy, anger, quarrels, dissensions, factions, envy, drunkenness, carousing, and things like these" (Gal. 5:19-21*a*). When these are ignored, it may result in a serious decline of the health of the church. The presence of these behaviors should call us to attention so that the health and strength of the church can be restored.

Biblical Ground Rules

1. *Giving and Taking Offense* (1 Cor. 8—11:1). In dealing with the cultural issue in Corinth the apostle Paul wrote, "If food is a cause of their falling, I will never eat meat, so that I may not cause one of them to fall" (8:13). He also wrote,

> "All things are lawful," but not all things are beneficial. "All things are lawful," but not all things build up. Do not seek your own advantage, but that of the other. . . . So, whether you eat or drink, or whatever you do, do everything for the glory of God. Give no offense to Jews or to Greeks or to the church of God, just as I try to please everyone in everything I do, not seeking my own advantage, but that of the many, so that many may be saved. Be imitators of me, as I am of Christ *(10:23-24, 31—11:1).*

The guiding principle of love instructs us to govern our lives for the good of our brother and sister. To intentionally offend is to violate another. However, it is also possible for the "weaker/offended" person to take offense where none was intended, to hold the "stronger/offending" person hostage to their sensitive conscience. Such manipulation is evil masquerading as weakness or superior piety.

The mature believer will seek not to offend and will not take offense where offense is not intended.

2. *Pride and Arrogance* (Acts 10; Rom. 12:3; Prov. 16:18; James 4:6-10). "God opposes the proud, but gives grace to the humble" (James 4:6). The account of Peter in Acts 10 is a model of God's humbling grace. In a vision from God to Peter, a large sheet was let down to earth by its four corners. It contained all kinds of four-footed animals as well as reptiles of the earth and birds of the air. "A voice told him, 'Get up, Peter, kill and eat.' 'Surely not, Lord!' Peter replied. 'I have never eaten anything impure or unclean'" (vv. 13-14, NIV). This occurred three times in succession for the purpose of emphasis. After contemplating the meaning of this vision, Peter found himself in a gathering of Gentiles. He confessed the meaning of the vision by the following: "You are well aware that it is against our law for a Jew to associate with a Gentile or visit him. But God has shown me that I should not call any man impure or unclean" (v. 28, NIV).

The people of God do not elevate themselves by virtue of superior morality or adherence to law. "Pride goes before destruction, and a haughty spirit before a fall" (Prov. 16:18). "For by the grace given to me I say to everyone among you not to think of yourself more highly than you ought to think, but to think with sober judgment, each according to the measure of faith that God has assigned" (Rom. 12:3).

In dealing with divisive issues, pride rises as a judgmental spirit that condemns the other person. The fully devoted follower of Jesus will be open to correction by God, as was Peter. Should it be necessary to correct a fellow believer, it should be done in a spirit of gentleness. "My friends, if anyone is detected in a transgression, you who have received the Spirit should restore such a one in a spirit of gentleness" (Gal. 6:1).

3. *Gossip* (James 3; Ps. 34:13; Eph. 4:29—5:2). The tongue is an instrument given us for the praise of our God and the encouragement of the brothers and sisters in the family of God.

> Let no evil talk come out of your mouths, but only what is useful for building up, as there is need, so that your words may give grace to those who hear. And do not grieve the Holy Spirit of God, with which you were marked with a seal for the day of redemption. Put away from you all bitterness and wrath and anger and wrangling and slander, together with all malice, and be kind to one another, tenderhearted, forgiving one another, as God in Christ has forgiven you. Therefore be imitators of God, as beloved children, and live in love, as Christ loved us and gave himself up for us, a fragrant offering and sacrifice to God *(Eph. 4:29—5:2).*

"With the tongue we praise our Lord and Father, and with it we curse men, who have been made in God's likeness. Out of the same mouth come praise and cursing. My brothers, this should not be" (James 3:9-10, NIV). Again in Ps. 34:13 we are admonished, "Keep your tongue from evil and your lips from speaking lies" (NIV).

Gossip poisons the well of conversation in a community. It is a ferocious spectator sport that requires nothing but the willingness to do another harm by speaking words that are destructive at worst and unnecessary at best. We call upon our people to guard their own words and to courageously stop gossip when given the opportunity.

4. *Judgmental Attitudes* (Matt. 7:1-5; Rom. 2:1-11; 14:1-23). These texts deal with judging the behavior of others. While we are called to recognize evil by its fruit and to be discerning in our choices, we are not

called to play God in regard to others. It is possible to speak the truth (as we know it) in love and leave judgment to God. The warnings of Scripture are clear: "Do not judge, so that you may not be judged. For with the judgment you make you will be judged" (Matt. 7:1-2). "Therefore you have no excuse, whoever you are, when you judge others; for in passing judgment on another you condemn yourself, because you, the judge, are doing the very same things . . . by your hard and impenitent heart you are storing up wrath for yourself on the day of wrath, when God's righteous judgment will be revealed" (Rom. 2:1, 5).

We urge our people to guard their hearts and to seek the cleansing of the Holy Spirit as the only cure for a judgmental attitude. The Spirit of God fills the heart with love that drives out judgmentalism.

5. *Anonymity* (Matt. 5:21-26; 18:15-20; Eph. 4:25-27; Gal. 2:11-14). The Bible calls us to deal with divisive issues face-to-face, person-to-person. Paul modeled this in a dispute with Peter in Gal. 2:11-14. He opposed him "to his face" (v. 11). When it is obvious that an issue pits one believer against another, face-to-face honesty is called for. If a mediator or arbitrator is needed, one should be sought.

When divisiveness in the community revolves around a larger issue, a responsible leader should be approached. Hiding behind anonymous notes and letters is not the way of the people of God.

Dealing with Divisiveness

Divisive issues fall into one of two categories—personal or corporate. Personal matters can usually be dealt with between two or three persons or families. If these parties can reach reconciliation early in the process, the church will be the better for it. Such disagreements, disputes or misunderstandings left unresolved can often spread into a larger church conflagration. Therefore, we encourage all responsible members to seek biblical resolutions early in the conflict and in the smallest setting of persons.

Personal Issues

The following are suggestions for resolving personal misunderstandings.

1. Read 1 Cor. 13, and go to the offending or offended party in a spirit of love, having carefully prayed for guidance. Seek to reach an understanding concerning the details from both perspectives. Ask first to hear the perspective of the other before offering your own perspective. Taking

the initiative early in the disagreement can keep the problem from growing. Matthew 5:23-24 says, "Therefore, if you are offering your gift at the altar and there remember that your brother has something against you, leave your gift there in front of the altar. First go and be reconciled to your brother; then come and offer your gift" (NIV).

2. Be cautious about the words chosen to describe your point of view or cause of frustration. Words such as "always" or "never" are too exaggerated. Proverbs 15:1 makes the contrast between gentle and harsh words: "A gentle answer turns away wrath, but a harsh word stirs up anger" (NIV). We are called to "[speak] the truth in love" (Eph. 4:15). It is true that "a word aptly spoken is like apples of gold in settings of silver" (Prov. 25:11, NIV).

3. Seek reconciliation through forgiveness. In the Lord's Prayer, we are taught to ask forgiveness of sins even as we forgive (see Matt. 6:12). Jesus follows this instruction with a note of explanation: "For if you forgive men when they sin against you, your heavenly Father will also forgive you. But if you do not forgive men their sins, your Father will not forgive your sins" (vv. 14-15, NIV).

4. Leave room for differences of opinion to exist. The goal of unity is not that all would have the same opinion but that all would have love for the other. The unity of the church is not based on the absence of differing opinion but rather on the presence of a reconciling spirit.

Corporate Issues

The following are suggestions pertinent to resolving corporate issues.

1. Always seek to maintain a positive attitude toward Christ's body, the church. Paul states in Eph. 5:

> Christ loved the church and gave himself up for her, in order to make her holy by cleansing her with the washing of water by the word, so as to present the church to himself in splendor, without a spot or wrinkle or anything of the kind—yes, so that she may be holy and without blemish. In the same way, husbands should love their wives as they do their own bodies. He who loves his wife loves himself. For no one ever hates his own body, but he nourishes and tenderly cares for it, just as Christ does for the church, because we are members of his body. . . . This is a great mystery, and I am applying it to Christ and the church *(vv. 25-30, 32).*

When we damage the people of God, we have damaged the bride of Christ. It is possible to be so engaged in winning a debate or defending our position that the cost to the church becomes secondary. Our words and deeds are our visible witness. The church takes shape in the world as witness to God by our love.

2. Face the issue. Don't deny it. Don't go underground with it. Bring it into the open with responsible Christians and in a nonvindictive attitude. When Paul had a problem with Peter,

> [he] opposed him to his face, because he stood self-condemned; for until certain people came from James, he used to eat with the Gentiles. But after they came, he drew back and kept himself separate for fear of the circumcision faction. And the other Jews joined him in this hypocrisy, so that even Barnabas was led astray by their hypocrisy. But when I saw that they were not acting consistently with the truth of the gospel, I said to Cephas before them all, "If you, though a Jew, live like a Gentile and not like a Jew, how can you compel the Gentiles to live like Jews?" *(Gal. 2:11-14).*

Confronting a divisive issue is necessary, but caution must be taken to do it with the right people, at the right time, in the right spirit, with the right motives.

3. Choose a responsible leader to help you bring resolution to the issue. If the issue concerns a pastor, go first to that pastor. If it involves more than one person, seek out a board member, a staff pastor, or another responsible leader in the congregation.

When Confrontation Is Needed

Ongoing sin in the life of a believer obstructs his or her walk with the Lord, threatens the unity and fellowship within the body, and ultimately weakens the witness of the church among nonbelievers (1 John 1:7; 2 Cor. 6:3).

Scripture therefore encourages believers to be concerned with each other's spiritual well-being and teaches them to confront in love where there is evidence of sin. We acknowledge the following biblical procedure for such confrontation (2 Cor. 11:29; Luke 17:3; Gal. 6:1):

1. If one has knowledge of ongoing sin in the life of a fellow believer, he or she should go in love and confront the individual in private (Matt. 18:15).

2. If there is no expression of repentance, he or she should repeat his concern for the spiritual well-being of the individual in the presence of two or three witnesses (v. 16).

3. If there is still no repentance, Scripture teaches that the matter should be brought before the church. In our current context, we interpret this to mean the leaders of the congregation (v. 17).

4. If there is still no evidence of repentance, Scripture teaches that the individual should be removed from the body and believers should break fellowship with him or her, until such time as there is genuine repentance (2 Thess. 3:4 ff.; 1 Cor. 5:11; Titus 3:10-11). We believe this to be an act of love, not an act of coldhearted exclusion. It is the means by which the church bears witness to its concern for the individual.

In addition to the above procedure, Scripture teaches that confrontation should be approached and carried out with an attitude of love, concern, and humility and should be motivated by the sincere desire to see repentance and restoration of fellowship. Reflecting Christ's grace and forgiveness, believers are taught to be quick to forgive when there is the genuine expression of repentance on the part of a fellow believer (Gal. 6:1; Matt. 18:21 ff.; Matt. 6:14-15; Eph. 4:32; Luke 17:3).

The same biblical principles and procedures for confrontation apply in attempting to resolve relational conflicts within the body. In such cases, Scripture indicates that it is the responsibility of the believer to go promptly to his or her brother or sister who has been offended (Matt. 5:23-24; Eph. 4:26-27).

Responsibilities of Church Leaders

1. The church is responsible to provide a forum for dealing with corporate issues of concern to all. Town meetings, listening posts, and corporate gatherings will be provided on a regular basis for airing issues of community concern.

2. Elected leaders will represent the congregation by being ears to congregational concerns. They are charged with bringing such issues to the attention of the governing board for discussion, resolution, and action. They are charged with seeking resolution, not taking sides or increasing the volatility of the issue.

3. Leaders are responsible for lowering the threshold of accessibility. They must be available to listen. Behavior that causes another to feel unimportant is unacceptable.

4. The perceived distribution of power may be intimidating to the person in the pew and may generate a sense of "I don't want to be a troublemaker." The labeling of people who deal with issues face-to-face as "troublemakers" is unacceptable. Our people are invited to express their concerns to the leaders of the church.

5. Communication is vital to the process of ownership and community. We must be clear in the portrayal of visions, plans, and processes of ownership. The lack of clear information often creates division—the very opposite of what we desire as a church.

6. We must grant permission for individuals to disagree. At such times it is important for those of differing opinions to see where they agree and where they continue to disagree. Each person should be willing to become part of the solution. It is wrong to expect leaders to be the solitary "fixers" of every issue. While we are a corporate body, we live in this body as responsible, accountable individuals.

Conclusion

Fellowship within the body of Christ is often broken when a member experiences pain inflicted by another believer. It is our desire to minimize such pain, to grow in the process of healing the pain, and to mature in our capacity to be peacemakers.

The guiding principle of the Christian walk is love. In Gal. 5:14-15, Paul states that "the entire law is summed up in a single command: 'Love your neighbor as yourself.' If you keep on biting and devouring each other, watch out or you will be destroyed by each other" (NIV). John Wesley spoke of holiness as the love of God expelling all sin. We call our people to the high standard of holiness in dealing with divisive issues. It is our desire that the world know we are Christians by the quality of our love for one another.

20

TRUST

I am still moved by the powerful words of John Wesley, quoted earlier in chapter 17 by Pastor Matthew—words that begin, "I dare not, therefore, presume to impose my mode of worship on any other," and end with the poignant, "Leave all opinions alone on one side and the other: only give me your hand."[1]

Throughout the quotation Wesley is demonstrating trust based on a common confession of Christ as Lord. The church is in need of such trust at several levels. The essence of biblical covenant relationships is found in the Hebrew word *chesed*. When people enter covenant, *chesed* is established between them—meaning that each has the right to expect certain behavior of the other in light of the promises made. Trust suggests that we intend to behave in certain faithful ways toward each other while expecting the same in return. The beginning assumption is peace, not conflict; trust, not suspicion.

Generational Trust

An older generation needs to trust the missional spirit of a younger generation as they seek to reach their changing world. The pessimism about the younger generation is not valid. Our youth are in touch with the same God who found us early in our lives and dreamed through us the church as it became under our leadership. In twenty-five years of service on the campus of a denominational university, I have never heard college students plotting the demise of their grandparents' church. They simply do not think about the preservation of the church we poured our lives into. They are thinking about the expansion of the church into the world. We are tending our aging homes in hopes of preserving them through retirement, and they haven't even considered settling down but are headed toward a succession of apartments that serve as the staging ground for their expanding lives. They are going somewhere. We've already been. They are planting trees. We want to pick fruit from what we've already planted. Life is different from our perspectives. We must trust the coming generation to do the work of God in the world—with the hope that our trust in them will engender the kind of mentoring relationship that will make them wiser than they otherwise will be.

A younger generation needs to trust the critical response of an older generation. We have lived long enough to see harm done, even when it was not intended. We know heresy when we see it. We know the danger of emotion without reason, and reason without emotion. We are a little cynical because Ecclesiastes has taught us that there is nothing new under the sun—so we suspect that the new is the old recycled. We are a little afraid—because we no longer have the power in the world we once had. Our nation is weaker, our denomination is shrinking in the states, our power to earn money has declined, our nest egg has shrunk, our kind of TV is relegated to one channel, and our music is almost gone. Technology has raced past us. You can text faster than we can think. The world unsettles us. So we react in ways that you interpret as opposition. Please don't. We want to trust you, but we'll need some assurance that you are open to hear our wisdom—even if you decide to do it your way.

University/Church Trust

The church needs to trust the Christian college to do its thought-work in a complex world. Colleges have labs, libraries, Web connections, access to the world's research, and think tanks. Colleges have professors who have dedicated their lives to the study of specific fields and are proficient at examining the findings in these fields through the lens of their faith. The Christian university is a unique place. Yet it is often under attack for the very act of investigating, researching, and exploring. Those who have already reached their final conclusion about creation, political party, the environment, social justice, economic theory, and other important issues make their demands that the university side with their position or suffer the consequences. They wish the university to be the defender of their position and to indoctrinate the coming generation with their ideas.

This strategy contains two fundamental problems:

1. The college years are essential to the human development process known as self-differentiation. This begins in adolescence and continues into early adulthood. In simpler terms, college students define themselves as different from their parents by exploring and adopting a worldview that makes sense to them. Attempts to corral them into a protected bubble of "thought incubation" would make rebels of most of them, especially the imaginative and thoughtful. College students wish to explore their world, ask the hard questions, test the things they've been taught, and reach conclusions for themselves. They want to own their faith, not be told it.
2. This kind of protective education would not be in a conversation with the rapidly changing world. It would instill fear of all that is new. We would quickly void the world of Christian scientists, politicians, educators, and thinkers. They would merely be "on the attack" or cocooned in cloistered communities of fear. The Christian university should be placing highly skilled, professionally trained, thoughtful Christians in every field of endeavor. To operate at this level requires that they be conversant with the latest theories, literature, and technology. We do the service of God a great disservice by keeping our students from exploring their world.

But it must also be said that the university must trust the church. Higher education is not an excuse for arrogance toward a local congregation, a homeschooled student, or a concerned parent. The student in the college classroom is the beloved child of a family and a church. They have invested much more in this student than the professor just learning his or her name. An appropriate partnership is called for. For a religion professor to say, "I'm here to dispel everything you learned in Sunday school," is both arrogant and disrespectful. For a science professor to embarrass a student who espouses the seven-day literal creation of a young earth is uncalled for. The professor cannot assume that everyone has the privilege of higher education. It is highly likely that a parent or pastor, given the same privilege of years of graduate study, might come to the same conclusion as the professor. For the educated professor to assume that this person should agree with him or bow to his opinion, without access to years of study, is an unreasonable assumption. Conversation is more appropriate than castigation.

How true it is that knowledge puffs up—and equally true that love builds up.

In the process of higher education, students often return home to their families and churches and report the most startling, disturbing discovery they have made at college. They unload that which has the greatest shock value. Why? They are self-differentiating. They are testing the old arrangement where they believed what was told them without testing it for themselves. In college, they begin to think seriously, to champion ideas. It is easy for the folks back home to draw rash conclusions that this college must be liberal/new age/unorthodox (pick your label) because of what the young freshman has just said. As a college president who has fielded these calls from concerned parents and pastors, I would urge you to engage the student in a deeper conversation. He or she wants to be an adult in conversation with you, not the child who is told what to think and what not to think. This is an invitation to conversation being offered you, not their final decision about reality. If you overreact, they will eventually stop talking with you about these things.

Yes, sometimes professors are not faithful to the church in their teaching. They need to be confronted. Yes, sometimes the ranges of opinions expressed are not in keeping with the thought of the church. The university must proactively deal with this. But it must also be stated that the local family and church has more than its share of sloppy theology, unorthodox thinking, and distorted doctrine. Both need careful correction. To operate from the prejudiced viewpoint that higher education is anti-Christian is to shrink God to our narrow opinions.

The Christian university exists in service to the church. It engages our youth when they are self-differentiating from their parents, defining themselves as their own persons, not clones of their parents. It is common for them to question, to resist, and to think freely. This is how one comes to possess his or her own thought and faith. The Christian university provides an environment rich with wise friends—in dorms, classrooms, libraries, counseling centers, gyms, ball fields, jam sessions, and cafeterias. The people who work in our colleges are believers. And the people who occupy our pews are believers. It's time we trusted each other.

Trust in the Nonessentials

If we are to have "in essentials, unity; in nonessentials, liberty; in all things, charity," the million dollar question is—what is essential and what is nonessential?

I would suggest the essential things include a saving experience in which the Spirit of God bears witness with our spirit that we are the sons and daughters of God. I would also include the core of Christian faith as expressed in the Apostles' Creed and the stated doctrines of the church. (For me this is my denomination's sixteen Articles of Faith rooted in historic Methodist and Anglican belief.)

And that's about it.

My nonessentials list is a lot longer—creation theory, political party, hawk or dove, role of government, method of befriending the homosexually oriented, church music preference, preferred eschatology, favorite authors, method of baptism, church architecture, budget priorities, whether there is one or three authors/chronologies of Isaiah, interpretation of Gen. 1, the death penalty, the right of a woman to preach (although this comes close to being an essential for me), social drinking, reading from the early church fathers, yoga, blessing pets in the church sanctuary, speaking in tongues, Catholic theology, real wine or Welch's at Communion, casual or coat-and-tie on Sunday, Left Behind opinion, national health care, and so on. I have my opinions about these things, and reasons for most of my opinions. I care about some more than others. I think these are important issues. But none of them call for de-Christianizing someone. None of them need to separate brothers and sisters in Christ.

I like to think of the day when God, in Christ, makes all things new. This great eschatological move will restore the heavens and earth as God intended them to be in creation. It will be God's last great creative move (I think—who knows?). We will be resurrected from the dust, delivered from all sin, and made complete in Christ. On that day, the creation debate will end. My guess is that we will all be utterly amazed, and our opinions will melt into worship of the Creator. Political party affiliations will seem trite as we recognize the King of kings and Lord of lords. God will probably chuckle and ask some of us where we got the idea that women couldn't preach and then call on a woman to bring morning devotions. But it won't matter—even to our Baptist friends—that she does. Sexual orientation will not matter, but the friendship they had longed for in the less-than-matured church will be perfected in the kingdom come. Wine may be served, and even good Nazarenes will drink it—without fear that any will be harmed by its consumption. The bonds within families will be loving, covenant-binding acts of devotion. I think those among us who dug in their heels over nonessential issues will finally be able to lay down the burden of needing to be right and will be able to embrace those they fought unnecessarily.

So why not now? Can we love enough to trust? Within the boundaries of unity in essentials, can we find grace and charity in the nonessentials? Can the kingdom begin to break in today?

21

how to CHOOSE *a* CHURCH

You have a choice when it comes to churches. I'd suggest three specific categories that most churches might fit into.

You can attend Safe Church with a safe pastor who will find the middle of the road and stay in it. You will not have any of your thoughts challenged. You will hear from the pulpit what you already think. The radical kingdom of God will be domesticated to fit your cultural prejudice and your convenient, uncomplicated lifestyle. The infusion of new ideas from science, politics, immigrants, minorities, or education will not be welcomed. The Scriptures will not be interpreted into the world that currently exists but will be used to defend the world as you already see it. Discussion will center on issues already resolved by popular opinion. Being noncontroversial will be the guiding principle of the church. Getting along will matter more than anything else. The instant someone is uncomfortable in a conversation, it will cease or be diverted. Disagreement is akin to sin in Safe Church. These congregations can be found everywhere. You can consume the bland religion found in the middle of the road at Safe Church. And you will be encouraged to smile and play nice.

You can also find a church that claims to have everything figured out—Final Word Church. This church is much bolder than Safe Church. It thrives on controversy and actually is bolstered by enemies. When Oprah says something unreligious or Congress passes disputed legislation, the sermon for the coming Sunday is set. They have the final word on all doctrinal, ethical, social, and political issues. All you have to do is sign the dotted line of the membership covenant, and they will give you your position on everything—every candidate, every new ethical issue that emerges, every controversial topic. A disciple is a dittohead. These churches declare a kind of biblical authority that places their opinion above Scripture, while quoting just enough select verses to make you think they are biblical. The pastor usually has an ego and needs to be viewed as the savior of the world, the fountain of all wisdom, the master of PowerPoint, and the martyr willing to take a stand on any and every headline issue. Final Word Church is growing. And its people tend to be judgmental, arrogant, and mostly angry at the world.

Or you can attend a church that is willing to wrestle with the tough issues—Maturing Church. You can sit at the table with fellow Christians who are willing to grapple with new emerging questions about faith in every realm of life. You will grow accustomed to hearing an issue discussed by Christians with different perspectives. You will quickly discover that good people can read the same Bible and reach different conclusions. You will be formed as a maturing follower of Jesus in a changing world. Your worldview will continue to develop as you study Scripture and live in a vibrant community. Your church will and should discomfort you at times. Your church will and should expose your arrogance. And reading the Bible will become the most disturbing thing you do, because this world is not aligned with the ways of God. You will find taking up the cross of Jesus to be painful. You will encounter issues for which the answers are not black-and-white—criminal justice, poverty, political systems, use of force. You will develop mental categories for unresolved issues. And you will sit on the same pew with people who do not think like you think but who could not be more brother or sister, because your unity is rooted in the redeeming love that binds you together in Christ. Your church will be filled with vibrant conversations and vibrant love. And the people of Maturing Church will continue to grow in likeness to Jesus, without avoiding the hard questions (like they do at Safe Church) or becoming arrogant in knowing (like they do at Final Word Church).

All these churches can be found in your community.

When asked about the church I belong to, I like to say that we are the theological heirs of a man named John Wesley. He experienced God as holy love that expelled sin, enabling him to be restored in the likeness of Jesus. This profound experience caused him to saddle a horse and ride into the world. He travelled with his Bible open on his lap, reading as he went. He believed the God of love he experienced had gone into the world ahead of him and was calling him to follow. This God was not hiding in doctrines or waiting behind closed church doors to be discovered and debated. This God was en route to redeem his creation from sin. Wesley was given the eyes of God to see children in factories needing education, the poor needing food and shelter, the debtors in prison needing money, the sick needing good medical care. Wesley saw the broken world through the eyes of a loving Redeemer. He was not afraid of this world or its ideas, even when it rejected and attacked his God. He was a curious lifelong learner. He wrote about health, money, estate gifts, economic theory, personal grooming, literature, politics, science, and the arts. He made friends among those who had differing Christian theologies, offering his hand of fellowship and a catholic spirit. Wesley did not think God in need of human defense but did think people in need of godly help. His life of loving service caused people to be interested in his doctrine of entire sanctification. They wanted to know about the God who could do this kind of thing in a man and prompt such a life of service. We are the heirs of a man who knew that propositional debate as the primary goal of religion could only divide, but holy love could unite.

This theological heritage is viewed by some as a slippery slope into the "isms"—liberalism, new ageism, paganism, and so on. Tolerance, they say, becomes the demon in the room, and before long, anything goes. I beg to differ. I believe Christianity has more to lose from a debate-centered, intolerant, judgmental, arrogant, enemy-making response to the world. If we follow this playbook, we may win the game on points, but there will be no one left in the stands with any interest in what we are doing.

I choose to belong to a people whose God is bigger than our current scientific findings, enabling us to go into the future with scientific wonder and exploration of the universe—a universe we are certain God created and sustains. I choose to belong to a people who know that love builds up rather than puffs up and who take their relational cues from the God who exists in the loving relationship known as Trinity. I choose to belong to a people confident that God will bring all things to completion in Christ, but between here and there is much open-ended freedom for God to act and respond to his creation. I choose to belong to a people who are known by their love more than by their ability to slice a heretic to shreds. I choose to belong to a people interested in God's fallen world of politics, economics, health, science, the arts, sexuality, power, and money. I choose to belong to a people with their hearts, hands, and minds opened to fellow followers of Jesus who see things differently while still confessing the faith delivered to the saints. I believe the family of God lives in a big tent with a God even bigger than the tent.

22

DIFFERENT STARTING POINTS

In resolving differences, the language used often reveals one's theological camp. Protestant Christianity has two primary ways of thinking about God and the Christian faith—Reformed Calvinism and Wesleyan-Arminianism. In case you haven't picked it up, I'm from the Wesleyan-Arminian camp. And in my following attempt to broad-brush these two ways of thinking, I admit my bias and recognize that some Reformed folks would describe themselves differently.

The Reformed-Calvinist thinkers had their origins in the Protestant Reformation. Martin Luther and John Calvin are significant historical figures to them, as to all of Christianity. Calvin was a lawyer whose precision with words, ideas, and propositional constructs was quite "lawyerly." Doctrinal proposition was important—getting it right.

Calvin's understanding of God centered on God's sovereignty. God is the all-powerful ruler over all. What God wills is done. How God intended history to play out is settled. What God's book says is without error of any kind and true. Good Calvinists are apologists. They argue proposition toward truth as an act of faithfulness to God. Defending the truth is the core of their work. Authority and power, as rooted in the sovereignty of God, are the currency of their religious system, and truth is the goal for all believers. When they do business with each other over disagreements, the categories are truth, falsehood, heresy, and orthodoxy.

The Wesleyan-Arminians also have their roots in the Protestant Reformation, but the significant historical figures are Jacobus Arminius and John Wesley. Wesleyans begin with the holiness of God and, in particular, the relationship that the holy God desires with his sinful creatures. The redemptive story of God's move in love to forgive and cleanse the creature and bring him or her into right relationship with him is the basis of the faith. Important to Wesleyans is covenantal theology, the relationship that God established with his people. The Hebrew word *chesed* denotes the behavior that each has the right to expect of the other in light of the promises made. Love is the primary currency of this religious system, and right relationships are the goal (right relationships between God and us, between each other, and with all creation). When we do business with each other over disagreements, our categories are love, respect, telling the truth, mercy, justice, the fruit of the Spirit exemplified, and Christlike behavior toward each other.

It strikes me that Wesleyans have begun to disagree in Calvinist categories. When issues such as evolution, emerging church, and alcohol find us calling each other heretics, false teachers, and inerrant-Scripture doubters, we have shifted camps from attention on relationships to a focus on propositions.

My guess is that the proper balance between Calvin and Wesley might be somewhere in the middle between the two. The tension between these two poles is sufficient to create a paradox. It's hard to play a tune on a limp fiddle string.

Truth is important, but truth at the cost of loving relationships is not Christianity. And relationships that ignore truth will lose integrity sooner or later.

23

a GRIEF OBSERVED

For Lent this year I have been reading Eugene Peterson's *Practice Resurrection: A Conversation on Growing Up in Christ.* He writes about his first pastorate and the desire to form a church where people would do two things: worship God and be formed into community.[1] Attending a neighborhood community meeting six weeks into his residency, he quickly learned that the people in his neighborhood were contentious, rude, and unwilling to even listen to each other. They did not like each other. These were the people who would be the church in this community. He was reminded of the phrase from Ps. 120 in the old King James Version, "Woe is me, that I sojourn in [Meshech], that I dwell in the tents of Kedar!" Meshech and Kedar were barbarian tribes with a reputation for wildness.[2] Here was a God-worshipper en route to the temple for worship who felt as though he lived not among brothers and sisters but among barbarians.

A good friend who leads a significant ministry recently said to me, "If I can retire still loving God and the church, it will be a miracle of grace." He, like so many other administrative church leaders, has been caught in the cross fire of competing demands.

I have found wonderful friends outside the church. Many of them have come to faith in God and are now in the church. But I had to protect them from much of what I was dealing with from within the church. Had they seen what I was going through, they would have never heard the gospel. They thought we loved each other and wanted to serve the community around us in the name of Jesus. Being with them was often my best Sabbath from the demands of the barbarians.

I do not close in pessimism, because I believe in the resurrection. Dead people can live again. Enemies can become brothers and sisters in Christ. I am hopeful. But the jihadist barbarians are on the move in the church today, and as long as they get their way, we'll need to protect the pagans from them.

24

the ROLE OF THE CHRISTIAN UNIVERSITY

The world has changed. The 9/11 terrorist attack did more to us than we know. It introduced us to a complexity that our powers had no way to confront. Used to fighting wars with enemies who appeared on the battlefield under opposing flags, we knew how to mass our forces against such enemies and gather sufficient armies to win. Now we face enemies who have no country, no flag, and no turf. They fight ideologically, defend no territory, and exist only by making enemies. They destroy without regard. They leave behind rubble with no intent to erect a better society to prove their point. They are willing to hold life hostage as a means of getting what they want. They live by instilling fear.

In many ways, we are living in the days of Solomon. Remember the woman whose baby died. She stole the child of another woman and appeared before the wise king to settle the opposing claims of motherhood. The woman who took the baby was willing to let the baby be divided with a sword rather than surrender her rights to it. Getting what she wanted was more important than the life of the child. The woman who wanted the baby to live was its true mother, but she was placed in an unthinkable situation of having to surrender the child to declare her love for it. The other woman was a terrorist. At any price, she wanted what she wanted, without regard for the life inherent in the child. Only the wisdom of Solomon brought sanity to the moment and gave the child to the one who was its true mother (1 Kings 3).

The discourse occurring in most denominations these days is taken from the playbook of terrorists and thieving mothers. Winning debates is more important than the creation of peaceful communities, more valued than the life of the children. We've seen the Baptists rend one another over women preachers and inerrancy debates and destroy their colleges and seminaries with litmus tests. We've seen the Episcopalians divide over the ordination of practicing homosexuals. We've seen Catholics divide over birth control, the role of women in the church, and clerical abuse.

I would not begin to suggest that these are not important matters that ultimately define religious movements. These issues need charitable discourse. But what we've seen is the rending of the body, the creation of enemies where brothers and sisters once embraced, and the eruption of uncivil discourse in the church. Conversations, as observed earlier, are like the childhood game pin the tail on the donkey. They end as soon as the donkey is appropriately pinned. Discourse goes only deep enough to attach labels.

How we debate our differences says as much about us as where we end up. The body of Christ is looking more and more like news talk shows that pit the extreme right against the extreme left for ratings. We are like Stephen Colbert with his arrogant one-liners or Letterman with his punch lines or Limbaugh with his smears. Discussions are nothing more than drive-by shootings. Technology permits such a discussion by way of blogs, Web sites, and fan pages. The one thing missing is bodies. Being people who embrace the doctrine of the incarnation, God becoming flesh, it seems that the church should at least have bodied conversations. Cybersmear never looks in the eyes of another person and beholds a creature of God. With terrorism or false mothers, bodies just don't matter that much.

Where in the world can one find a discussion on important issues that is two-way, listening as well as speaking, civil, informed, and willing to suspend judgment while studying the complexity of the issues? Where in the world is Christian faith delving into difficulty with eyes and ears open to the fact that complex issues are not easily resolved? Where is civil discourse happening? Where are people disagreeing with one another without becoming sworn enemies? Where is increasing knowledge being balanced by growing wisdom? Where is the trained thinking of the church gathered for the purpose of tending to the thought life of its youth?

I would suggest that the Christian university is the site of such an undertaking. In chapter 20 I mentioned several things about the Christian university, its relationship and responsibility to the church, and the efforts of some groups who seek to impose their will on it. But now I want to bring forward something we looked at in chapter 21, that we are theological heirs of John Wesley. Our heritage means many things for Wesleyan-Holiness universities, but mostly it means that we educate from the perspective of a Wesleyan worldview.

1. We believe God engages us across the entire liberal arts curriculum. We speak of God as quickly in a science or history class as in a religion class. God's revelation is not limited to the university chapel. We believe there is a biblical way to understand political power, economic theory, public school education, science, the human body, and the use of technology.

2. We prepare students for life in the middle of the world. We do not shield, protect, or coddle them in an unreal spiritual bubble. Rather, we declare that God has gone into the world ahead of us and is calling us to follow. True discipleship can only be fulfilled by following God into that needy world. Saints aren't made behind closed church doors or defensive doctrinal positions. We believe it is possible to live in the world without being of the world. It is important to us that our students are interested in the world rather than afraid of it. Like Wesley, they travel with a Bible on their lap, interpreting the world through the revelation of God.

3. We place high emphasis on the development of the whole person. We are made to love God with body, mind, soul, and strength. The practices of spiritual formation are important to us—prayer, fasting, Scripture study, hospitality, listening to God in silence, Communion, and worship. These habits form us as Christians. Our students study, laugh, play, and eat—and sometimes sleep. They are involved in clubs, classes, intramural athletics, dramatic productions, and campus social life. Our dorm life is an extension of the academic classroom because there we learn respect for property, problem solving, relational integrity, sharing, and all the other values that help us live peacefully in a community.

4. We also believe that holiness is highly relational. The mentoring relationship between university employees and students is essential to a Wesleyan education. We learn from each other. Years later, it is not so much content as godly influence that is the abiding gift of a Christian university.

5. We learn in an academic atmosphere that is hospitable and charitable to those who do not believe as we do. Wesley called it a catholic spirit. A profession of Christian faith is not required for one to attend our colleges. Having our ideas challenged is part of the educational process. We are not afraid of asking the hard questions or debating the difficult issues. What better place to work through doubts and questions than a campus filled with godly mentors?

25

the LITMUS TEST

I am intrigued by litmus tests. There are several definitions.[1]

Litmus test: a common chemical pH test that indicates whether a solution is acid or alkaline: red indicates an acid solution; blue indicates an alkaline solution.

Litmus test: any kind of social indicator used to classify someone either favorably or unfavorably.

Litmus test: in politics, a question asked of a political candidate, the answer to which determines support or opposition.

Litmus test: a crucial or revealing test in which there is one decisive factor.

Litmus test: a test that produces a decisive result by measuring a single indicator.

I'd like to find the one thing, the one characteristic, the one reality, the one indicator, the one revealing factor that tells me I am in the presence of a holy person.

I believe the litmus test of a holy person is perfect love as defined in Scripture and embodied in the life of Jesus.

Scripture is most clear on this:

> I give you a new commandment, that you love one another. Just as I have loved you, you also should love one another. By this litmus test [my translation of the Greek there] everyone will know that you are my disciples, if you have love for one another *(John 13:34-35)*.

But loving one another isn't the end of it. The writer of 1 John adds in 4:7-21,

> Beloved, let us love one another, because love is from God; everyone who loves is born of God and knows God. Whoever does not love does not know God, for God is love. [Sounds like a litmus test to me.] God's love was revealed among us in this way: God sent his only Son into the world so that we might live through him. In this is love, not that we loved God but that he loved us and sent his Son to be the atoning sacrifice for our sins. Beloved, since God loved us so much, we also ought to love one another. No one has ever seen God; if we love one another, God lives in us, and his love is perfected in us. By this we know that we abide in him and he in us, because he has given us of his Spirit. [Litmus test?] And we have seen and do testify that the Father has sent his Son as the Savior of the world. God abides in those who confess that Jesus is the Son of God, and they abide in God. So we have known and believe the love that God has for us. God is love, and those who abide in love abide in God, and God abides in them. Love has been perfected among us in this: that we may have boldness on the day of judgment, because as he is, so are we in this world. There is no fear in love, but perfect love casts out fear; for fear has to do with punishment, and whoever fears has not reached perfection in love. We love because he first loved us. Those who say, "I love God," and hate their brothers or sisters, are liars; for those who do not love a brother or sister whom they have seen, cannot love God whom they have not seen. The commandment we have from him is this: those who love God must love their brothers and sisters also.

First John also tells us that this especially includes a brother or sister in need.

And one more text—Matt. 5:43-48:

> You have heard that it was said, "You shall love your neighbor and hate your enemy." But I say to you, Love your enemies and pray for those who persecute you, so that you may be children of your Father in heaven; for he makes his sun rise on the evil and the good, and sends rain on the righteous and on the unrighteous. For if you love those who love you, what reward do you have? Do not even the tax collectors do the same? And if you greet only your brothers and sisters, what more are you doing than others? Do not even the Gentiles do the same? Be perfect, therefore, as your heavenly Father is perfect.

Perfect love includes our brothers and sisters, those we see in need, and even our enemies—and it is all based on the way that we have been loved by God.

Even with its theological shortcomings, the poplar book *The Shack*[2] gives us an interesting picture of Trinity talking at the table one evening. There is a natural love flowing between Father, Son, and Spirit. I like to think that the holy life is getting caught in the middle of this love triangle and breathing it in and out, offering it to others, and being fully shaped by it. We are called to receive and live from the love of God.

The litmus test of a holy person is perfect love.

But I'm not sure this is the litmus test anymore—the one thing, the one characteristic, the one reality, the one indicator, the one revealing factor, the defining thing that tells me I am in the presence of a holy person.

I've seen several different litmus tests—the emerging church, evolution, creation theory, age of the earth, worship style, version of Scripture, political party, budget formula, response to homosexuality, Obama, Catholics, yoga. I'm sure you have yours to add.

Remember the definition: "Litmus test: any kind of social indicator used to classify someone either favorably or unfavorably."

Things have changed.

Two cultural realities concern me. Both have to do with the way we relate to each other.

My first concern is consumerism. Martin Buber[3] called it the "I–it" relationship. In this way of relating, we turn people into objects and use them. We relate primarily on the basis of what we might get. We become a world of consumers with goods to be bought and sold. We run on greed —the desire to profit from each other by the transactions we have.

For example, I am interested in you because I am a college president and you are a budget-paying pastor. I treat you nicely because I want you to sit in a board meeting and persuade your recalcitrant members to pay the college budget.

Or the college student is interested in dating that girl because she will enhance his image, provide a sexual partner, or make his ex-girlfriend jealous.

Or you meet your neighbor because you sell insurance and she might be a prospect. People you would normally ignore are suddenly on your radar screen.

We all know what it is like to be treated as an object, an "it" to be used. Our interest in each other is transactional. Remove the transaction, and there is no relationship.

Now this is not all bad. If my tooth is abscessed, I want to have a transaction with a dentist who also wishes to profit from me. I didn't call him up to get to know him. But the problem is that this way of seeing each other has become so dominant that we don't see people.

This has leaked into the church for thirty years now. I think it started with the homogeneous unit principle, where we concluded it was easier to reach people who were like us, people with the same consumer tastes. And it is. Then came the seeker movement targeting felt needs. We got good at marketing. And these seeker churches became megachurches who figured out how to franchise the gospel in multiple locations through technology and reach more consumers of religion.

It's not all bad. It is how we are being shaped by our culture. And soon, we start thinking about church differently. We see people in a different way. We tell them we have the hottest band, the coolest youth program, or the youngest old folks group in town. Whatever "it" wishes to consume, we provide.

You want short sermons, our preacher is up and down in twenty minutes.

You like loud, we do that at 11:00 AM.

Soft? We can do that at 9:00 AM.

Fun youth group? Our teens did a work and witness trip at Disney World last summer.

Tithe? How does 7.5 percent sound?

Controversy? No problem. We stick to the safe middle of the road so as not to negatively affect our consumer base.

We please to the max.

You are probably holier than I am, but I must confess that as a Christian living in a consumer world, I find this way of relating sneaking into my tired soul. Love is so demanding. Using people is a lot easier.

Do pastors ever look at the congregation and see "program-doers"? Or worshippers who should like their new favorite style of music as much as they do? Or donors for the newest idea? Or feeders of their ego? Or participants in their codependency? Or approvers of their unhealthy work ethic? Or backslappers following the Sunday sermon? Or problems in the flesh angling to triangle them to one side of an issue? Do pastors see "its"?

One time I was trying to move a congregation to love lost people the way God does. They didn't want to. And they were acting out. So I ramped up the octane because they wouldn't consume my new outreach program and go get their lost friends. I planted motivational zingers in the Sunday sermons and made heroes of the people who were on board. And then by the middle of the next week I was griping and whining to God about these people who wouldn't open wide and swallow what I was dishing out. And God reminded me, "I love found people too." So I apologized for treating them like pawns instead of people.

This cultural reality can start making you see

a crowd instead of a face
a number instead of a name
a prospect instead of a person

Has this ever happened to you?

Perfect love is not only the fruit of sanctification but also the litmus test of a holy person. Do you actually love people? See them as God sees them? Tell them the truth? Do what is best for them in the sight of God?

There is a second cultural reality that seems to be gaining on consumerism as a primary way of relating to people. Martin Buber called this the "us–them" relationship.[4]

We were shocked into this way of relating by 9/11. President Bush identified the axis of evil, telling us who and what to hate. American politics, both right and left, learned that you win elections by naming the enemy and making people afraid of what the enemy is trying to do to you. Common hatred is now the tightest glue that bonds people together. It is the world of jihad—holy war.

Jihad is a process of declaring who is "us" and who is "them." Jihad has a strategy. It declares itself the authority and interprets the text to justify its position. Jihad is right. Then it names the enemy. Then it gathers a group of followers by instilling fear of what the enemy is trying to do to them. Then it attacks.

There is no middle ground—only "us" and "them." It is practiced regularly on talk radio, political TV, branding ads, billboards, social media, and slanderous jokes circulated on the Internet. Negative branding is the means by which we create "them." "Them" can be lots of folks:

Greedy bankers who caused the economic meltdown
President Obama
The Democrats—The Republicans

Those tree-hugging, environmental whackos
Al Gore and his global-warming pals
The Catholics who pray to Mary
The Baptists who won't ordain women
The Methodists who drink socially
The Episcopalians who ordain practicing homosexuals
The Independents who won't join a denomination
and pay budgets like all God-fearing Christians are supposed to
The professors who teach evolution
The emerging church

Whatever the issue, there is "us" and there is "them." The litmus test is your position on the issue, and this single thing becomes for you the indicator used to classify someone either favorably or unfavorably.

If the "I–it" relationship runs on greed, the "us–them" relationship runs on fear. Eugene Peterson writes in his recent book *Practice Resurrection*, "When tactics of fear are used in Christian communities to motivate a life of trust in God and love of neighbor . . . habits of maturity never have a chance to develop."[5]

Our Scriptures tell us that "perfect love casts out fear" (1 John 4:18). We are to love our enemies, not attack them. Enemy love is a litmus test of the people of God. We are called to act toward our enemies as God acts toward his enemies.

Most of what I see happening in the "us–them" relationships is anything but loving. It is arrogant, puffed up, judgmental, and unkind; it impugns motives, castigates leaders, nitpicks statements, and belittles holiness. And it is all done out of the fear that we may be getting too tolerant of these folks.

While tolerance is considered a virtue, I'm not suggesting that tolerance should be our goal. I'm suggesting that we go far past tolerance to perfect love. Don't stop at tolerating "them," actually love them. Practice in loving one's enemies is often hard to come by.

So how do we live in a consumer-oriented, jihadist world? We practice love perfected, love expelling all sin, love of God with heart, soul, mind, and strength, love of neighbor as self.

Martin Buber calls it the "I–you" relationship.[6]

I am my brother and sister's keeper—that's you. And you are my keeper. We are neighbors. We are children of a common Creator whose

Son died a sacrificial death on a historical cross for every one of us. We are called to treat each other the same way God in Christ has treated us.

If we could bug the dining room of the Trinity, what do you think we would hear? How do you think the Father speaks to the Son, or the Son to the Spirit, about scientists who have differing theories of the origin of creation? About Democrats and Republicans? About Catholics and Episcopalians? About emerging church leaders, and contemporary worship leaders? About homosexuals? About Muslims? Imagine eavesdropping on a divine conversation within the Trinity about these people. I doubt there would be labeling or hatred or fear or belittling. I'd guess there would be holy love.

We are brought together into a covenant relationship of "I–you." What binds us together is *chesed*, a Hebrew word that means "what each of us has the right to expect of the other in light of promises that have been made."[7]

Now you may think I would be in favor of some kind of mushy middle where all of us think alike. That would be most boring and is highly unlikely. The church would become very small if everyone totally agreed with me—or you. In this church of perfect love, there is unity around Christ. And unity has plenty of room for diversity.

Diversity runs deep in our theology. The Trinity is one God, three persons. Jesus is fully human, yet fully God. The Scriptures are divinely inspired, yet written by humans. Diversity is deep within our faith.

Did you know you can be a Christian and

be a Democrat or Republican
believe the earth is very young or believe the earth is billions of years old
think modern or postmodern
be emergent or nonemergent
be traditional or contemporary
wear ties or jeans to church
root for the Florida Gators or the Ohio State Buckeyes
(yes, God can handle this level of diversity in his family).

You can have voted for Obama or McCain and be a Christian.
You can be for or against troops in Afghanistan.
You can be for or against a nationalized health care program.
You can worship loudly or softly.
You can sit on pews or folding chairs or the floor.

You can read from the KJV, the NIV, the NRSV, the NLT,
or The Message.
You can recite ancient creeds or not.
You can be premillennial, postmillennial, or amillennial,
and maybe even unmillennial.
You can be dunked, sprinkled, or poured and be a Christian.
You can love a book or find it useless.
You can believe God created the earth in seven literal days or that
he created it through evolutionary processes across time
—and still be a Christian.

You can worship God in a dimly lit room with candles burning
and religious art on the walls
and prayer stations surrounding you
or
you can worship God in a room filled by organ pipes
and punctuated by stained-glass windows, robed choirs, and a big pulpit
—and still be a Christian.

But you cannot use and hate your fellow humans and be a Christian. You cannot persecute, defame, attack, or demean them. It doesn't matter if they are the president of the United States, a professor in a university, a leader in the church, a political candidate, a businessman in your town, a member of your congregation, a relative in your family, or your spouse—because the litmus test of a Christian is perfect love. And perfect love behaves like Jesus.

Friends, the church has a lot to discuss. The topics are before us, and divisiveness is occurring around many of these topics. I'm all for holy conversation. John Wesley included holy conversation as a means of grace to help us mature in likeness to Jesus.

My concern for the church is that we may become so embroiled in the debates and controversies of our day that we change the litmus test from perfect love to our position on an issue.

The church needs leaders. If you want to be distinctively Christian in this world, live out the doctrine of perfect love. Let this way of relating identify you. Love your brothers and sisters as Christ has loved you. Love your enemies.

It is a calling so massive that only a work of grace that we call entire sanctification can enable it. And our God is faithful. He will do it.

In essentials, unity;
in nonessentials, liberty;
in all things, charity.[1]

NOTES

Page 4

1. Attributed to Peter Meiderlin. See *Wikipedia,* s.v. "Rupertus Meldenius," http://en.wikipedia.org/wiki/Rupertus—Meldenius (accessed October 13, 2010).

Preface

1. Alexander Pope, *An Essay on Criticism,* pt. 3, line 66. See *Bartleby.com,* s.v. "Alexander Pope," http://www.bartleby.com/100/230.html (accessed October 13, 2010).

2. Attributed to Abraham Lincoln. See *QuoteWorld,* s.v. "Abraham Lincoln," http://www.quoteworld.org/quotes/8321 (accessed October 14, 2010).

3. Attributed to Francis of Assisi. See *ThinkExist.com Quotations,* s.v. "St. Francis of Assisi quotes," http://thinkexist.com/quotation/preach_the_gospel_at_all_times_and_when_necessary/219332.html (accessed October 14, 2010).

Chapter 2

1. M. Scott Peck, *People of the Lie: The Hope for Healing Human Evil* (New York: Simon and Schuster, 1983).

2. MusicalSchwartz.com, "Joel Grey, 'Sentimental Man,' and 'Wonderful'-lyrics, etc.," http://www.musicalschwartz.com/recordings/grey.htm (accessed October 28, 2010).

3. Ibid.

4. Ibid.

Chapter 3

1. Dan Boone, "Calling Down Fire from Heaven on the Health Care Bill," Dr. Dan Boone, posted April 12, 2010, http://www.drdanboone.com/?m=201004 (accessed July 20, 2010).

Chapter 6

1. For a fuller discussion of Revelation, see Dan Boone, *Answers for Chicken Little* (Kansas City: Beacon Hill Press of Kansas City, 2005).

2. From an outline provided by Dr. Tom Noble. The address was given in 2010 to the district superintendents of the Church of the Nazarene in Florida. Dr. Noble is currently writing a systematic theology for the Church of the Nazarene.

3. Eugene Peterson, *Working the Angles: The Shape of Pastoral Integrity* (Grand Rapids: William B. Eerdmans, 1987), 107.

Chapter 9

1. This sermon was preached in the Trevecca Nazarene University chapel service during the heat of the 2008 election, won by Obama. The campus poll was almost evenly divided between the candidates.

2. John Ortberg, *The Life You've Always Wanted: Spiritual Disciplines for Ordinary People* (Grand Rapids: Zondervan, 1997), 17.

3. Martin Luther, "A Mighty Fortress Is Our God," trans. Frederick H. Hedge (1852).

4. Maltbie D. Babcock, "This Is My Father's World" (1901).

Chapter 10

1. Statistics from "Alcohol Statistics," Alcohol Info, http://www.alcohol-information.com/Alcohol_Statistics.html; "Alcohol Use," Centers for Disease Control and Prevention, http://www.cdc.gov/nchs/fastats/alcohol.htm; and "Alcohol Statistics in the United States," AlcoholAlert, http://www.alcoholalert.com/alcohol-statistics.html (all accessed October 14, 2010).

Chapter 11

1. A sermon preached in chapel at Trevecca Nazarene University (October 16, 2007).

2. Raniero Cantalamessa, *Contemplating the Trinity: The Path to the Abundant Christian Life* (Ijamsville, MD: Word Among Us Press, 2007), 82.

Chapter 12

1. See the argument in the chapter on alcohol for a closer look at the issue in Corinth.

Chapter 14

1. Karl Giberson and Darrel Falk, "We Believe in Evolution . . . and God," *USA Today,* August 17, 2009, http://blogs.usatoday.com/.a/6a00d83451b46269e21020a4dc71ee970b-pi (site no longer accessible).

2. Noble, outline of 2010 address to district superintendents.

3. Denis Alexander, *Creation or Evolution: Do We Have to Choose?* (Oxford: Monarch Books, 2008), summarized in Noble, 2010 address.

4. Francis Collins, *The Language of God: A Scientist Presents Evidence for Belief* (New York: Free Press, 2006), 200.

5. Ibid., 233-34.

6. Saint Augustine, *The Literal Meaning of Genesis,* translated and annotated by John Hammond Taylor, S.J. (New York: Newman Press, 1982), 1:41.

7. John H. Walton, *The Lost World of Genesis One: Ancient Cosmology and the Origins Debate* (Downers Grove, IL: IVP Academic, 2009).

8. Ibid., 96.

9. B. B. Warfield, *Selected Shorter Writings* (Phillipsburg: PRR Publishing, 1970), 463-65.

Chapter 15

1. Dan Boone, *The Worship Plot: Finding Unity in Our Common Story* (Kansas City: Beacon Hill Press of Kansas City, 2007), 10.

2. Ibid., 7-8.

3. Tom Noble reviewed the three books referenced in his 2010 address to Church of the Nazarene district superintendents. This summary is used with gratitude for his permission.

4. Eddie Gibbs and Ryan K. Bolger, *Emerging Churches* (Grand Rapids: Baker, 2005), summarized in Noble, 2010 address.

5. D. A. Carson, *Becoming Conversant with the Emergent Church* (Grand Rapids: Zondervan, 2005), summarized in Noble, 2010 address.

6. Mark Liederbach and Alvin L. Reid, *The Convergent Church* (Grand Rapids: Kregel, 2009), summarized in Noble, 2010 address.

7. Scott Daniels, posted on NazNet.com from a blog, http://www.naznet.com/community/showthread.php?1631-The-Emergent-Church-is-Still-Dead (accessed October 15, 2010). Daniels is senior pastor of Pasadena First Church of the Nazarene, Pasadena, California. In the same blog he writes, "I wish I was the first one to make this declaration, but I'm not. Michael Patton and Anthony Bradley have already written nice obituaries for the Emerging Church [http://online.worldmag.com/2010/04/14/farewell-emerging-church-1989-2010/ and http://www.reclaimingthemind.org/blog/2009/05/obituary-the-emerging-church-1994-2009/]."

8. Ibid.

9. Ibid.

10. Ibid.

Chapter 16

1. See my book *The Worship Plot.*

2. "Brian D. McLaren: Denominations do invaluable things," Faith and Leadership, http://www.faithandleadership.com/multimedia/brian-d-mclaren-denominations-do-invaluable-things.

Chapter 17

1. Editor of *Holiness Today* magazine for the Church of the Nazarene. Felter has taken criticism for his balanced approach to the issue of the emerging church.

2. John Wesley, "Catholic Spirit," in *The Works of John Wesley,* 3rd ed. (London: Wesleyan Methodist Book Room, 1872; repr., Kansas City: Beacon Hill Press of Kansas City, 1986), 5: 496-99.

Chapter 18

1. The first two are found in the work of Benjamin Barber, *Jihad vs. McWorld: How Globalism and Tribalism Are Reshaping the World* (New York: Ballantine Books 1995). Dean Blevins offers Table Conversation as the Christian response to these pedagogies.

2. The remainder of this chapter, including this paragraph, is an adaption and expansion of section C, "Invitation to the Dance," in *The Worship Plot,* 113-23.

3. Reginald Heber, "Holy, Holy, Holy" (1826).

Chapter 20

1. John Wesley, *The Works of John Wesley* (Kansas City: Beacon Hill Press of Kansas City, 1978), 496-99.

Chapter 23

1. Eugene Peterson, *Practice Resurrection: A Conversation on Growing Up in Christ* (Grand Rapids: William B. Eerdmans, 2010), 133-36.

2. Ibid., 136.

Chapter 25

1. Sources: *Dictionary.com,* s.v. "litmus test," http://dictionary.reference.com/browse/litmus+test, and *Wikipedia,* s.v. "Litmus (disambiguation)," http://en.wikipedia.org/wiki/Litmus_%28disambiguation%29 (all accessed October 14, 2010).

2. William Young, *The Shack* (Newbury Park, CA: Windblown Media), 2007.

3. Martin Buber, *I and Thou,* trans. Ronald Gregor Smith (New York: Charles Scribner's Sons, 1958).

4. Ibid.

5. Peterson, *Practice Resurrection,* 252.

6. Buber, *I and Thou.*

7. Author's definition.

Page 183

1. Same as note 1, page 4.

What readers are saying about *A Charitable Discourse . . .*

"*A Charitable Discourse* encourages and challenges me to commit to the consistent practice of holy conversation."

—Douglas S. Hardy, Professor of Spiritual Formation
Nazarene Theological Seminary

"Dan Boone has given us a careful look at complex issues through the unique lens of Wesleyan theology."

—William Greathouse, General Superintendent Emeritus
Church of the Nazarene

"There will be some who will read it with their jaws on the floor and do the complete opposite of everything [Boone] talked about. Others will quietly ponder for the rest of their lives. Some will dive right in and begin conversations before they even finish the book. For many, it will save their lives."

—Ashley Gernand, Congregational Worship Leader

"He treats the topics in the context of both academic and practical thought and research."

—Nina G. Gunter, General Superintendent Emerita
Church of the Nazarene

"Boone presents for the reader a clear path for Christian discourse vital to the current generation of believers."

—Sidney Gholson, Layman
Murfreesboro, Tennessee

"*Charitable Discourse* is a needed and timely message for today's Christ-followers."

—Bob Brower, President
Point Loma Nazarene University

"In a day when shrill and insensitive voices parade as intelligent public discourse, Christians need to recall that in the Body of Christ, a patient love that 'builds up,' not a zealotry that eliminates diversity, evidences the Spirit of Christ. Dan Boone maps this better path."

—Al Truesdale
Author of *The Baal Conspiracy, God Reconsidered,* and *God in the Laboratory*

"*Charitable Discourse* is a call to remember who we are as the holy people of God, called to walk in his character. If we ever needed *Charitable Discourse,* we need it now!"

—Edwin H. Robinson, President
MidAmerica Nazarene University

"The book does what it proposes . . . it initiates a conversation."

—Greg Mason, District Superintendent
Louisiana District, Mississippi District

"I will recommend this book to our pastors, and I will do it without reservations or a disclaimer. In fact, I may buy it for them."

—Ron McCormack, District Superintendent
Eastern Tennessee District

"An educator par excellence . . . I recommend this book for study and consideration."

—Roy E. Rogers, District Superintendent
Georgia District

"A younger generation is waiting and watching in hopes of finding an 'honest, mature conversation to join.' This book will help us 'bring them in.'"

—E. LeBron Fairbanks, Education Commissioner
International Board of Education, Church of the Nazarene

"Have you wanted to converse with others in authentic and transparent ways about complex and controversial issues? Are you ready to be invited to the table of civil discourse? If so, this is the book for which you've been waiting. I commend this book to all Wesleyans willing to learn from one another."

— Eddie Estep, District Superintendent
South Carolina District

"Dan Boone has written a book that finally addresses some of the vexing issues that face the Christians of our day in a very honest and readable way."

—Howard T. Wall III, Senior Vice President and General Counsel
Capella Healthcare

Let's talk about it!

A CHARITABLE DISCOURSE

You've read *A Charitable Discourse.* Now go further in your discussions by engaging with the *Small-Group Version*. Filled with weekly discussion topics, Dan Boone's *Small-Group Version* leads people to develop well-thought-out discourse.

www.BeaconHillBooks.com

FIND **FREEDOM** IN THE COMMANDMENTS

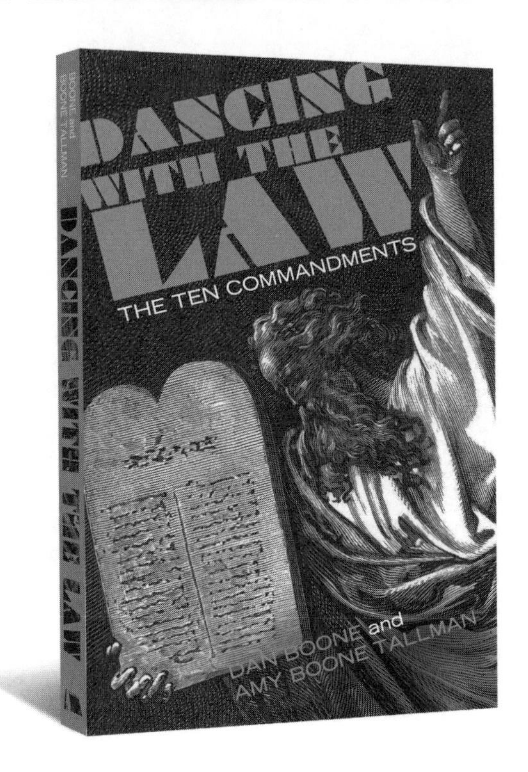

In *Dancing with the Law,* authors Dan Boone and Amy Boone Tallman challenge us to—like the ancient people of God who revered and celebrated law—look at law as a sacred gift that points the way to the life God intended for us. Through this earnest exploration of the Ten Commandments, they offer us a new perspective on law—one that makes us dance with freedom, liberty, and the gift of life.

Dancing with the Law
The Ten Commandments
Dan Boone and Amy Boone Tallman
ISBN 978-0-8341-2491-2

Available online and wherever books are sold.